MILLENNIAL
LEADERS

Success Stories From Today's
Most Brilliant Generation Y Leaders

BEA FIELDS, SCOTT WILDER
JIM BUNCH & ROB NEWBOLD

NEW YORK

MILLENNIAL LEADERS

By Bea Fields, Scott Wilder, Jim Bunch & Rob Newbold

ISBN: 978-1-60037-350-3   **Paperback**

ISBN: 978-1-60037-351-0   **Hardcover**

Library of Congress Control Number: 2007938655

Published by:

MORGAN · JAMES
THE ENTREPRENEURIAL PUBLISHER™

Morgan James Publishing, LLC
1225 Franklin Ave Ste 325
Garden City, NY 11530-1693
Toll Free 800-485-4943
www.MorganJamesPublishing.com

Cover Wrap & Interior Design by:

Heather Kirk
www.GraphicsByHeather.com
Heather@GraphicsByHeather.com

Front Cover Concept by:

Raluca Ciuperca
Retina Web Agency

NOTE FROM THE AUTHORS:
We are proud to be able to donate 15% of all book profits to The Glimpse Foundation, a 501(c)3 nonprofit that fosters cross-cultural understanding and exchange, particularly between the United States and the rest of the world, by providing forums for sharing the experiences of young adults living and studying abroad.

» TABLE OF CONTENTS «

» PREFACE «

The Language of Generation Y

In the late 90s, when I was teaching classroom after classroom full of Gen Y students at New York University, I was struck by two things: wow, these kids have drive and, boy does their way of speaking jar my ear sometimes.

I'm Dr. Patricia Ross. I'm an English professor by training, and I had the pleasure of looking at this manuscript before it went to publication. It seems there was some concern about the language. Some said the writing was too "choppy." As I looked at a few interviews, it confirmed my hunch. It might read "choppy" to some because this is how Gen Yers talk. They have grown up on a steady diet of sound bites and short quips, and their ability to text message — the art of punctuated short speech — is astonishing. But it doesn't lead to a kind of language that older ears are used to.

Does that make it wrong? No, absolutely not. They may have short attention spans and the "instant" in instant gratification is far faster for them than it is for us slower moving Gen Xers and Baby Boomers. But these young people have amazing energy and a strong sense of commitment to good cause — just to name a few of their good traits.

So, if you are a Gen Yer and are reading this — pay no attention to the professors. We're just quibbling because while we might not understand the way you talk, we are keen to know what you're talking about.

Y If you're like me, a Gen Xer, or part of the older generations —
the Boomers and the 'Silent Generation' — then I challenge you
to read this with an open mind — and a forgiving ear. The people
who you are going to read about are amazing by any generational
standard, and since these people are our future leaders, it is important to pay attention to what they have to say!

Read past what might jar. Learn who these incredible people
are. If you're like me, you'll find yourself cheering them on in their
efforts. They are making great strides in making this world a better
place to live — for all of us!

Patricia Ross, Ph.D.
www.BestAffirmations.com

» ACKNOWLEDGEMENTS «

As with any project, writing a book is not a solo act. We want to thank the following people for their hard work, dedication and long hours to making this a fabulous project.

Sue Publicover, Corey Blake and the Writers of the **Round Table Inc** Team for managing this entire authoring process with such passion and a commitment to excellence. You are truly first class pros!

Dr. Patricia Ross for the final editing and writing a wonderful preface to *Millennial Leaders*.

Dale and Becki Noles of Virtual Accuracy for managing the **Gen Y Project** podcast and website.

Lisa McElmurry for transcribing over 30 hours of audios into written interviews.

Ann Fields for her insight on writing the chapter "Points for Reflection."

To those professionals who connected us to our team of experts:

Lori Richardson	Frank Ball
Pam Krulitz	Corey Blake
Rob Newbold	Michael Simmons
Jan Gordon	Scott Wilder
Dave Buck	Arel Moodie
Bert Gervais	Lisa McElmurry

Y And finally, to the experts who are represented in this book. We thank you for sharing your knowledge with our team and for taking the time you took to review and edit your chapters. We would not have this brilliant book without each and every one of you.

» PART ONE «

The "What" of the Y

Y

» CHAPTER 1 «

The Roots of a Generation

*"Here is a generation of young adults who have
never been without the Internet or cell phones. The
Soviet Union existed only in their history books. To
'Google' is a verb and text messaging is their email."*

Echo Boomers. The Connecteds. Generation Y. Millennials.
This isn't a list of rock bands, but the numerous names
attached to the generation of young people who were born after
1980. And there are 74 million of them in the United States right
now, a population that will soon outnumber the Baby Boomers who
have dominated the workplace for two generations.

These are the babies of the Boomers and they are making an
indelible mark on our society. In sheer numbers, Gen Y is a force to
be reckoned with. In addition to the population size of this group,
they bring to our culture a new set of behavioral standards that have
led them to become vastly successful as entrepreneurs. They are also
far more cause-driven than any generation that has preceded them.
Coupled with their unflagging confidence, technological superiority, and indomitable self-esteem, Gen Y is a cultural phenomenon.

Let's put this in perspective. Here is a generation of young adults
who have never been without the Internet or cell phones. The
Soviet Union existed only in their history books. To "Google" is a
verb and text messaging is their email. They have been able to
watch wars live on television, although they probably switch the

channel to one of the reality shows — neither is new for them because they never lived without such programming.

Gen Y, as a group, has tremendous influence in our culture, with a powerful impact on the workplace. On the job, they are interacting with members of other generations — Gen X, Baby Boomers, and the Silent Generation. Each generation brings its own perspective and set of traits, but how do you bridge the ever-widening gap between so many interconnecting age groups?

That was the question that confronted us time and time again as professional coaches. As we explored the answer, we began to recognize a palette of intriguing characteristics that prevail among the Gen Y. Some of these traits presented a distinct advantage to succeeding in the business world. Their belief that anything is possible fuels their drive to be entrepreneurs, and they're starting their enterprises as early as grade school. Technology has been ingrained in their lives since birth, empowering them with an incredible access to and command of the latest advances, in contrast to other generations who are still struggling with the media that comes so naturally to Gen Yers.

We also discovered that the newest group of employees has been raised to feel entitled. Over-involved parents have given them such heightened self-confidence that they are completely unaware of certain realities. The reliance on the Internet and text messaging to communicate within their social networks has reduced many social and interpersonal skills. They have great expectations and an "I want it now" impatience that confounds their managers and employers.

As the issue of Gen Y's effect on the workplace appeared to fuel a chronic concern of Generation X, Baby Boomers, and the Silent Generation, we decided to take our professional interest farther. We began speaking with people who have focused their careers on generational studies. We contacted successful Gen Yers who are making a difference in their worlds, using their passions and skills to be leaders for their peers.

As our stash of fascinating insight continued to grow, we saw the need to share it with others who have been unable to find a way to live, work, and play with these unique youth. In this book, we offer perspective on the upbringing that has created the Gen Y mindset by letting the experts speak for themselves. We deliver their knowledge and advice to help you grasp the core essence and unrealized potential of this segment of the population.

If you are a Gen Yer, you'll discover how to connect with your elders in the workplace. You'll learn what sets you apart from others and why your experience doesn't always meet your expectations. You'll hear from members of your generation who have turned their passion into a tangible result, and focused their enormous energy and spirit into transforming their lives into something more meaningful than a job. You will most certainly become less confused about colleagues and managers outside your generation; you might even uncover a new source of learning in their collective wisdom.

For our readers who belong to the other generations in today's workforce, you are about to learn that the young men and women from Generation Y are not intentionally trying to challenge you. They come from a totally different perspective, with mores that we — as parents, teachers, coaches, and bosses — instilled in them. Our efforts have given them their distinct character but we are left wondering how to effectively manage these individuals. As you read the commentary of seasoned experts on generational differences, you'll realize that you're not alone in your frustration and confusion. Join the rest of the country's employers who are struggling to fit these unique individuals into an outdated culture — and learn how to take a more productive route to finding, hiring, and retaining these job-hoppers.

Chapter by chapter, we will reveal more insight into the mindset of Gen Y. You'll learn what makes them tick, how to get into their network, gain their loyalty and respect, and why this generation can and will shift our culture. As the largest population of consumers since the Baby Boomers, Gen Y will soon dictate what products will be successful. They will influence the way businesses market their products and services, forcing a whole new advertising genre that has to deal with savvier, less loyal, and impatient consumers.

This book is about busting myths, not people. Gen Y has been accused of being self-serving, lazy, and disrespectful. We'll explore the realities of these myths, revealing a generation of young people who are dedicated to volunteerism and making a positive change in their world. We'll show you that these highly self-sufficient individuals welcome leadership and respect the value of older mentors.

Different times have made this generation remarkable in many ways. They're going to lead and respond in a manner that is foreign to people who have followed the traditional set of rules for workplace behavior and career development. We ushered in a new millennium. It makes sense that this new age brought with it a shift in the social currents. Call them Gen Y, Millennials, Connecteds, or Echo Boomers. The names vary but the tremendous potential of this generation demands consideration. As a business person, you can look back at the old days and the old ways, or you can lead in a brand new way from a position of understanding this next great generation.

The journey thus far has been enlightening, invigorating, and inspiring for us. We invite you to share these discoveries and experience so many of the "aha moments" that have shed new light on this intriguing shift in our world population.

» CHAPTER 2 «

"Generation Me": Dr. Jean Twenge

"These kids didn't raise themselves. They're doing what they were taught to do — from parents, teachers, and a lot from media."

A person can be defined by many factors. The science of genetics, the geography of your upbringing, and even the metaphysics of astrology contribute to who you are and how you are viewed. From a cultural perspective, the period in which you are born and raised makes a great impact on your being. The world changes from one generation to the next, with technology, events, and sociology shaping each group.

Gen Y is as unique as those generations that came before them and those that will follow. Dr. Jean Twenge has spent years studying the unique character of the Gen Y segment. Her research has appeared in *Time*, *the New York Times*, and the *Washington Post*.

As a professor of psychology, author of *Generation Me*, and a living, breathing Gen X/Y hybrid, Dr. Twenge is an authority on what makes a Gen Y tick. What causes them, as a group, to be impatient, overconfident, and to set unrealistic expectations? Why is it that Gen Y thrives on a social network that doesn't rely on face to face relationships? Dr. Twenge has examined the parenting style that brought these young people to believe that anything is possible — even when it isn't.

While Dr. Twenge takes a microscopic view of Gen Y, she also steps back to provide the bigger picture as to what these unique individuals can offer. She shared with us valuable insight on ways that older generations can best work with this growing population as it is beginning to saturate our businesses, institutions, and organizations.

Gen Y Project:

Jean, how did you become so interested in learning about "Generation Me"?

Dr. Twenge:

I'm a Gen Xer by birth; I was born in 1971, although our generation didn't have a name until the early 90s. I noticed that all the books I read didn't have much data on these individuals and their personality traits.

When I got to graduate school, I decided to look into this. There were cultural changes that would have an effect on people so they would have different personalities depending on the generation. Seeing that pattern in the things I'd done and then trying to find more data, that's what really got me into it.

Gen Y Project:

Your research shows that high expectations are one of the hallmark traits. Some might view this as a negative, but wouldn't you agree that a goal-oriented mentality and high expectations are necessary attributes for success?

Dr. Twenge:

We're brought up with this phrase "you can be anything you want to be." The problem is, that phrase just isn't true. There are certain limits. It's fine to encourage kids to have high goals, but now we're encouraging them to have widely unrealistic goals.

Gen Y Project:

So we just need to be more realistic here and be sure that our children are confident in their talents as well as aware of their limits?

Dr. Twenge:

It's not that we shouldn't encourage kids; it's that they should have the right goal for them based on their talents and abilities. This idea that we should encourage kids to aim for the stars — we should, but within reason.

Gen Y Project:

I would think that confidence is a positive trait. Is it just a matter of too much of a good thing?

Dr. Twenge:

A lot of these young people think they're going to get promoted quickly and rise to the head of the company by the time they're 28. Sure, it does happen, but they think it's common and it's not. A lot of managers said kids come in and don't want to work for it. They want it all right now. They get into the job and find out it's not absolutely everything they thought it was going to be.

Gen Y Project:

So how do we effectively correct their expectations?

Dr. Twenge:

Not being realistic in our feedback actually does more harm than good. We have this idea that we shouldn't criticize people because it will damage their self-esteem and then they'll give up. That's not actually how it works. Success tends to come first and that builds their self-esteem.

Gen Y Project:

So, the ability to accept criticism contributes to success, in effect, building your emotional and mental muscles. Now, Dr. Twenge, there are other workplace issues you've studied. The fashion attitude of Gen Y doesn't always conform to the standards of a business environment, does it?

Dr. Twenge:

As for dress, the need for social approval has gone. You have to make the rules very clear and also explain why there is this standard in the workplace. With a Gen Yer, you have to tell why it will be good for them. They want to be successful, and when they understand that what they wear plays into that, they get it.

Gen Y Project:

Although individuality fosters creative, fresh ideas, there are certain areas where conformity is the better option to support a company's culture. We're also hearing that job-hopping is common among Gen Y. Why is that?

Dr. Twenge:

Loyalty is a quality that is very unrecognized with Generation Me. It's about "what can you do for me, and if you don't give it to me, I'm going to leave." They'll keep job-hopping to try to find the job that fulfills all of their very high expectations.

Gen Y Project:

So how does a business owner encourage a Gen Yer to be part of a team?

Dr. Twenge:

It has to be something where the roles are clearly defined. They're working in a group, but they have an individual job and they can be more accountable. Then again, just emphasizing the benefits to them of working in a group makes a difference. They don't just want a job; they want it to mean something.

Gen Y Project:

How does social responsibility compare with their desire to succeed financially?

Dr. Twenge:

In October 2006, a poll of 18 to 25 year-olds asked them what their most important goal was. Number one was getting rich: 81% said that was an important goal; 51% said becoming famous was an important goal. Only about 30% said helping someone who needed help, about 20% said becoming leaders in the community, and only about 10% said becoming more spiritual.

Gen Y Project:

So spirituality isn't key to this generation?

Dr. Twenge:

There's been research done by a number of people on this generation and religion. Fairly uniformly, they find that this generation is significantly less religious than those that came before it. When you ask them why, they'll say that they don't want to "follow all the rules" so they're doing what they've been taught: to be an individual.

Gen Y Project:

How do they form their sense of morals?

Dr. Twenge:

There is much more of a reliance on the individual rather than social rules. For example, more than one-third of babies today are born to women who are not married. That's one social rule that has fallen by the wayside.

Gen Y Project:

How different is our impression of Gen Y versus our parents' impression of us?

Dr. Twenge:

Each generation thinks the next generation is more narcissistic, but apparently they're right. This generation is so much more narcissistic. Asking a Generation Me member to put duty before self would be like asking an American to become Chinese: it's all about culture. There are different cultures around the world, as well as different cultures around generations. These kids didn't raise themselves; they're doing what they were taught to do — from parents, teachers, and a lot from media.

Gen Y Project:

In your book, you discuss how the fantasy and reality aren't matching up. What issues occur as a result?

Dr. Twenge:

Anxiety and depression are up among this generation. There are a lot of different reasons behind those statistics; stress is one of them. Another is probably the lack of social connections. More people are lonely and don't have the close social connections of previous generations.

Gen Y Project:

But a lot of social networkers will counter that they have over 500 people in their Facebook account. How do you respond to that?

Dr. Twenge:

How many are real live friends? If you're just spending time on the computer and aren't spending time with people face to face, it ends up being something that makes you less mentally healthy.

Gen Y Project:

More face to face interactions would add joy and connection to your life, at any age. Dr. Twenge, we've been focusing on some of the negative attributes of this generation. Can you share some of the positive traits you've identified?

Dr. Twenge:

I would argue that the biggest one is tolerance and a pretty blasé attitude around issues involving race and gender. It's not a big deal for a woman to pursue a career, for example, and it's not a big deal that the black kid down the hall is the smartest kid in the dorm. It's not something they even really process. That's the upside of "do what's right for you." It can mean freedom, and we're not going to worry about somebody's background.

And obviously, they're tech savvy. They are open to a lot of different ideas, and they might end up being more creative because they've been taught to be unique and stand out.

Gen Y Project:

This openness to diversity opens the door for a broader range of experiences and interactions. In addition, these young people are technically savvier than their elders, they are narcissistic, and they are driven to suc-

ceed. With all these traits, can we expect that Gen Y will seek help to fill in the gaps of their shortened experience and knowledge?

Dr. Twenge:

They do seek out help. It sounds so paradoxical, but they almost expect parents to help them and serve them. The same is probably true of seeking mentors in the workplace. They want help from other people. Now, whether they take the advice or not, that's another thing.

POINTS FOR REFLECTION

The members of the innovative Gen Y can learn a great deal from the study and analysis of Dr. Jean Twenge. Here is some advice for you:

 A goal-oriented mentality and high expectations are necessary attributes for success in any situation. However, be realistic. Success usually doesn't come overnight. Be confident in your talents, know your limits, and when success doesn't come instantly, be patient!

 The ability to accept and embrace criticism allows you to improve and succeed. People fear that criticizing someone will damage one's self-esteem, when in reality providing honest, open feedback can actually help build mental and emotional muscles and support people in reaching their full potential.

 Individuality inspires creativity and fresh ideas in the work force, and certainly makes you stand out. However, sometimes conformity is the best decision for yours and others' sake. By understanding and following your company's culture (including things such as dress code and communication methods), you will find that you can strengthen your relationship with your colleagues.

 Being open to diversity and aware of other cultures will allow you to interact with a wide variety of people, and can help open the minds of senior colleagues. Learn to integrate this new age cultural awareness with the wisdom and experience of elders, and success will follow.

 Be aware of your emotional state. In the culture of Generation Y, stress and loneliness are common emotions, largely due to the emphasis on achievement and Internet use for social interactions. By relaxing and having more face to face interactions with people, you will add joy and connection to your life.

ABOUT DR. JEAN TWENGE

Jean M. Twenge, Ph.D., is Associate Professor of Psychology at San Diego State University and the author of *Generation Me*. You can find more about her and her research at <u>www.jeantwenge.com</u> or <u>www.generationme.org.</u>

Y

» CHAPTER 3 «

Next Generation Consulting:
Rebecca Ryan

"We dream about the day when all people—not just the next generation—can feel fully engaged and really turned on by where they live and work."

There was a time, not so long ago, when an individual found a job and then relocated as needed. Gen Y has dramatically altered this standard. In their mindset, a fulfilling lifestyle is more important than the job, which, in their view, is likely to be a short-term commitment — to the chagrin of many employers. As a result, the members of Gen Y select the location first and then focus the job hunt in that area. Meanwhile, workers from the older generations who simply adapted to their career requirements rather than dictating them are simply scratching their heads, trying to make sense of this new standard.

In reality, other generations can learn a great deal from Gen Y's shift in priorities. By understanding what motivates their thinking, we can begin to communicate, recruit, and retain new hires, and also to consider adjusting our own thinking to enhance our lifestyles.

Rebecca Ryan of Next Generation Consulting has spent years analyzing the behavior of this intriguing generation. Being on the cusp of Gen Y, she has close ties to, and a true fascination with, the mores that have shaped a new culture. Rebecca's passion is in teaching the leaders of today how to engage those of the future.

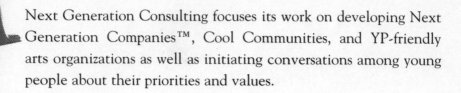

Next Generation Consulting focuses its work on developing Next Generation Companies™, Cool Communities, and YP-friendly arts organizations as well as initiating conversations among young people about their priorities and values.

Gen Y Project:

This whole issue of building a new generation of leaders has been heightened by the gradual exodus of Baby Boomers from the workplace. The next generation, Gen X, seems to be a much smaller population, so the numbers just aren't sufficient enough to fill the leadership gaps in the workforce. Now we're looking at Gen Y, and trying to find a way to fill the widening workplace gaps with twenty-something leaders whom we know think, act, and work differently from other generations. What do business, corporate, and community leaders need to be considering regarding making this generational shift in the workplace?

Rebecca:

To begin, I would like to talk about two factors that are creating a storm around this issue. One is that the economy has shifted and, for the United States to compete, we have to be an innovation-based, knowledge-based workforce. About 20 percent of the current workforce is college graduates working in knowledge-based occupations. That number just needs to go up in order to fill this gap. A lot of companies are competing for a finite pool of highly skilled workers.

The second issue is that the next generation behaves, operates, calculates and values differently. Our research is teaching us that where young professionals live is as important as where they work.

Gen Y Project:

So, business leaders need to hone in on a knowledge-based workforce and consider the fact that Gen Y is looking closely at not just where they work, but where they live. That is interesting. I know when I graduated from college, I looked at the career options first, not really considering the city I lived in. Gen Y is certainly exhibiting a mindset shift compared to two decades ago.

Rebecca, what motivated you to focus your career on understanding next generation thinking?

Rebecca:

I was a honked off Gen Xer, born in 1972 and raised by traditionalists. Growing up, I had a lot of messages about what it meant to be a loyal employee. Five years after I graduated from college, I felt like a miserable failure because I'd had five jobs in four years; my parents thought I was an alien life form. They couldn't understand how I could do all this job-hopping. Then at my class reunion, we were talking about our career paths and all of us had had multiple jobs. I thought, "I'm not the only weirdo who's looking for something more in a job," and I wanted to understand why.

Gen Y Project:

Where did you go from there?

Rebecca:

When I started in 1998, I was really focused on helping companies become great employers for the next generation. I was hired by companies to figure out why the tech-savvy talent left, in the hopes they could turn that into a framework for keeping them in the future. I did around 3,000 interviews and came up with what I call "drivers of engagement."

Gen Y Project:

Got it. You uncovered what was really motivating these talented young men and women to stick with a job. What a valuable breakthrough! What are these drivers?

19 «

Rebecca:

These six drivers are things that engage the next generation of knowledge workers:

1 **Voice**. They want to have a say in their work and how their work gets done.

2 **Membership**. They say they want to feel like they're part of something bigger.

3 **Meaning**. They want to feel like they're working for something more than just the bottom line. This is why the socially responsible organizations are attracting the young workers.

4 **Life/work balance**. Many employees feel that if they take the benefits that are provided to them — even the time that's allotted — they can be penalized at work for having a personal life.

5 **Enrichment**. Young professionals want to have the tools, technology, and training to do their jobs well and to grow.

6 **Appreciation**. Managers are so pressed to operate for results that they're forgetting that the art of management is really about motivating the people around you.

Gen Y Project:

Part of the premise of your book is that Gen Yers are choosing cities first, and work second.

Rebecca:

Yes, and let me say I am hearing this on both sides of the generational aisle. I recently had a conversation with the president of a community college whose daughter had just gotten an accounting degree. When he was talking with her about where she was looking for work, she named places she wanted to live, not companies to work for.

Gen Y Project:

It appears that your research supports this trend.

Rebecca:

We surveyed young professionals and discovered that three out of four under the age of 28 said where they live matters more than where they work.

Gen Y Project:

So with location as the primary motivator, those companies with attractive locations have the upper hand when it comes to recruiting talent. I imagine your framework also includes a means to measure the appeal of cities.

Rebecca:

Whenever we work in a city, we do a handprint of it, which is a community score on seven indices.

Gen Y Project:

Can you give us a breakdown of those indices?

Rebecca:

*Absolutely. The first is **vitality**. This is the community's commitment to the environment — we look at parks, trails, recreation areas; we look at recycling; we look at whether there is a farmer's market so they are able to eat fresh fruits and vegetables.*

*Next is the **earning index**. The question is about the breadth of occupational options. Are there lots of options or is there basically one employ-*

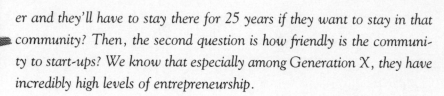

er and they'll have to stay there for 25 years if they want to stay in that community? Then, the second question is how friendly is the community to start-ups? We know that especially among Generation X, they have incredibly high levels of entrepreneurship.

The next is the **learning index**. A lot of urban centers are struggling with K-12 education and that's a major turnoff for young families. Second is lifelong learning options for adult learners. You know, young people may, at some point, change careers. This is where communities like Boston, which has 25 colleges or universities in its metro area, place high.

Then there is the **after-hours index**. What's there to do after 5:00? A writer for the alternative newspaper in Charlotte, North Carolina, picked the best bookstore, movie theatre, jazz club, etc. He drove to all of those places in one night, and had to put 33 miles on his car. Charlotte's got all these after-hours things but they don't have them clustered. We call them "stroll districts," a place where you can park once and walk to everything.

The next one is the **"around town" index**. We're measuring how much time people spend in traffic, the commitment to public transportation, if people carpool, if the community is multi-modal, meaning you've got protected bike lanes, bike and blade lanes, and so forth.

Gen Y Project:

That's interesting. What is it about the "around town" index that makes it so important?

Rebecca:

We know that if people have an easier time getting around to work, if the community is multi-modal, citizens tend to be more engaged.

Gen Y Project:

Got it. And what are the last two indices?

Rebecca:

The second-to-last is **cost of lifestyle**. *Can I afford to live here? Nashville gets pretty great marks in cost of lifestyle. There are some communities like San Francisco and Seattle, where it's more expensive to live, but the interesting thing is that even in the communities that are seen as expensive, it's not enough to discourage young professionals from moving there. It's not enough to be great in one index. All seven indices matter.*

Finally, we use **social capital** *to describe how rich the social fabric is in a community. When we think about a rich social fabric, we think of a community where all talent can be included. So we look at things like whether your community has an active young-professionals organization. What is the role of African-Americans in your community? Columbus, Ohio, has an incredibly large number per capita of people of color who hold executive positions and high-level management positions. Atlanta is the same way, and these communities tend to attract lots of young professionals regardless of their creed or color or lifestyle.*

Communities that include everybody are places where the next generation wants to live. It's because our college campuses look more like the United Nations. These people want to live in communities that reflect the diversity that they've learned is valuable.

Gen Y Project:

Based on everything we know about Gen Y, this set of indices makes sense, but how receptive are Gen X, Baby Boomers and Traditionalists to this scale?

Rebecca:

One of the things you run into when you start talking to those people about these indices — and they're mostly from my dad's generation or people who share his values — is that all we have to do is provide jobs and these people will come. Our comeback is that yes, you do have to be thinking about jobs because the earning index is one of the things a young professional will look at, but the counter-argument is that with the amount of things that happen digitally today, people don't have to move to your community to contribute to your employer's value proposition. People telecommute, people work online.

Gen Y Project:

There's such a competitive spirit about retaining talent. Do companies feel pressured to deliver on all the motivators as well as these geographic indices, hoping to keep the A players around? We have heard a great deal about how common job-hopping is with Gen Y.

Rebecca:

Yes, they do feel pressured to deliver a variety of motivators and incentives. And yes, Gen Y is known for job hopping. The constant exodus of talent is very expensive for organizations to replace. This is an investment in getting your company to grow and retain top talent.

Gen Y Project:

What closing thoughts do you have for our future workforce and for all generations?

Rebecca:

To encourage all people — not just the next generation — to look closely at how they can be fully engaged and really turned on by where they live and where they work.

POINTS FOR REFLECTION

 As you are considering a career, it's important to look at the full picture of your life. Life is not just about work. It's about living a rich and rewarding experience. Consider choosing a city that will offer you a satisfying cultural, educational and social environment.

 If you are working with a great company and you are interested in living in a different city, speak with your employer about working from a remote location. Because of advances in technology, it is now possible to work from almost any location in the world.

 As you are building out your career, get "plugged into" your city by getting involved in local community organizations and participating in volunteerism and philanthropic causes. Visit your local area Chamber of Commerce, local library and Convention and Visitors' Bureau to find out what community opportunities are available for young leaders.

 If your community is lacking opportunities for young leaders to connect, take the steps necessary to start a YPO (Young Professionals Organization). For more information, visit http://www.YPCommons.org.

 If you are living in a small community, make a list of every attribute you have and consider how you can use your skills and talents to support your small community in being all that it can be. Remember: Larger cities and states rely on the strength of small cities in order to prosper, and your contributions can help small towns grow and thrive.

Note: If you are a Gen X, Baby Boomer or Traditionalist, we want to encourage you to visit http://www.NextGenerationConsulting.com

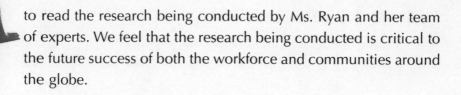

to read the research being conducted by Ms. Ryan and her team of experts. We feel that the research being conducted is critical to the future success of both the workforce and communities around the globe.

ABOUT REBECCA RYAN

Rebecca Ryan is one of the 2EO's of Next Generation Consulting, a market research company committed to engaging the next generation. She was named "Entrepreneur of the Year" by the U.S. Association for Small Business and Entrepreneurship and "Communicator of the Year" by Women in Communication. She is the author of the book *Live First, Work Second*. For more information on Rebecca or her book, visit her online at www.NextGenerationConsulting.com.

» CHAPTER 4 «

RainmakerThinking, Inc.: Carolyn A. Martin, Ph.D.

"Without a doubt, Gen Y is the highest maintenance workforce in history. They want feedback <u>now</u>, they want training <u>now</u>, they want recognition <u>now</u>, and they want to create the lifestyle they desire <u>now</u>. If managers can learn how to harness their energy and coach them effectively, these young employees have the potential to be the highest producing generation ever."

Right now, every industry in America is going through a dramatic "changing of the guard" called the Generation Shift™. Traditionalists are streaming out of the workplace; Baby Boomers are redefining aging and retirement; Gen Xers are the next generation of leaders; and Gen Yers have become today's fastest growing workforce.

Together, Xers and Yers comprise 52 percent of the workforce and bring to the table needs and expectations that often baffle older, more experienced professionals.

Over the past 15 years, Gen Xers have shown they are not averse to job-hopping in order to create the career and lifestyle they want. So, it's not surprising that their younger siblings in Generation Y are doing the same. How do we engage the interests of this young workforce so we can reap the benefits of their energy, talent, and productivity for years to come?

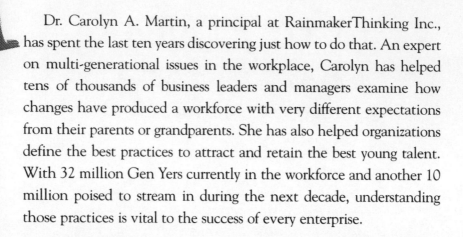

Dr. Carolyn A. Martin, a principal at RainmakerThinking Inc., has spent the last ten years discovering just how to do that. An expert on multi-generational issues in the workplace, Carolyn has helped tens of thousands of business leaders and managers examine how changes have produced a workforce with very different expectations from their parents or grandparents. She has also helped organizations define the best practices to attract and retain the best young talent. With 32 million Gen Yers currently in the workforce and another 10 million poised to stream in during the next decade, understanding those practices is vital to the success of every enterprise.

Gen Y Project:

What are some of the specific changes in the workplace that shape the ways Gen Xers and Gen Yers approach work?

Carolyn:

Perhaps the most significant change is the demise of job security. When Traditionalists (born before 1946) and Baby Boomers (1946 to 1964) entered the workforce, they thought they'd pay their dues, climb some-one's ladder, and cash out at retirement. That belief evaporated in the early 90s when organizations had to get lean and mean and let thousands of loyal employees go. At that time, Gen Xers (1965 to 1977) were entering the workplace and saw Baby Boomers hiding under their desks, begging, "Don't downsize me. I've put in my time. I've been loyal." And they heard organizations say to those Boomers, "Don't take this person-ally, but we have to let you go."

Gen Y Project:

Yes, I remember how painful it was for many of the Boomers to be cut loose.

Carolyn:

Absolutely! They grew up thinking organizations would take care of them if they were loyal. However, that all changed as the marketplace became more fiercely competitive and technology and globalization began to drive business decisions.

As a result, Gen X became the first generation to know from day one of their working lives something we all know today: There's no such thing as job security. For them — and for Gen Yers (born after 1977) — security lies in their own ability to amass marketable skills they can take wherever they go. You can't rely on a job — or even an organization — to be there tomorrow.

Gen Y Project:

What kind of impact has this self-reliant attitude had on organizations?

Carolyn:

It means a huge shift in how managers have to supervise people of every age. The old world of long-term benefits for long-term sacrifices is gone. Today, everything is short-term. Young people are asking: "What can you offer me today? What value can I add today? How can I build my career today? What can I learn today? What problems can I solve today? What meaningful work can I do today?"

And, understand that "short-term" for Gen Yers is really short! A year is an illusion for them. Right now is their reality!

Gen Y Project:

I've spoken with many managers from older generations who are struggling with the way Gen Yers approach work. They're frustrated with the "I want it all now" mindset that doesn't fit into their norm. What advice can you offer them for dealing with this generational gap?

Carolyn:

First of all, Gen Yers are the "education is cool" generation. They've been told by their parents, teachers, and counselors that education is the key to success, and they believe that. When you consider the U.S. Census Bureau report that says a person holding a high school diploma makes an average of $29,448 a year, while someone with a bachelor's earns $54,689, and those with a masters or above make $79,946, it's a compelling financial argument.

And, given their facility with technology, Gen Yers are poised to be life-long learners. For managers, this means making training and development an organizational obsession. Gen Yers will get bored and start updating their resumes if they stop learning.

Gen Y Project:

But what about the data from the Department of Education that says 45 percent of college freshmen drop out after the first year? What does this say about the "education is cool" generation?

Carolyn:

Not every young person wants or needs to go to college. I meet leaders from the "trades" all the time who say that hundreds of thousands of skilled laborers will be needed in the near future, but they can't be found. They tell me the salary a young person can make in the trades is often much more than they will make in a white-collar job. So high school counselors need to balance this push to go to college with other options for Gen Yers. But, of course, they'll have to convince Baby Boomer parents that it's all right. White collar or blue collar, the point still is that Gen Yers will want to keep learning and updating their skills.

Gen Y Project:

What impact do rapid technological advances have on training and educating Gen Y?

Carolyn:

This generation grew up with technology that was much more sophisticated than that used by previous generations, and they expect organizations to remain current in this. They don't see the latest technology as a luxury but as a business imperative.

Here's a great example. I was working with management majors at a large Midwestern university. They told a group of local business leaders that they expected laptops and cell phones as part of a job offer. The older pros were taken aback by a "demand" that the students viewed as a business necessity. The Gen Yers wanted to stay connected and be able to work from home after hours. The students were astonished by the inability of these older folks to differentiate between a perk and a productivity tool.

Richard Riley, the former director of the Department of Education, says that the top 10 jobs projected for 2010 didn't exist in 2004. That means we are preparing students for jobs that don't yet exist, using technology not yet invented, in order to solve problems we don't even know are problems yet. So, one of the best "perks" we can offer Gen Yers is a flexible work environment where they can capitalize on their ability to learn new things quickly with the technology to do that.

Gen Y Project:

What else characterizes Gen Y in the workplace?

Carolyn:

They are the "entitlement generation." Managers tell me these employees come in on day one and expect to have jobs out of whack with their experience, to assume leadership positions when they haven't proven themselves, or to be given a blue ribbon just for participating — like they were rewarded for playing on the soccer team without scoring a goal.

Gen Y Project:

Where does this entitlement attitude come from?

Carolyn:

Parent and teachers, mostly. One college senior explained, "They told us we can do anything, so we feel entitled to go in and have some opportunities to show what we can do with our skills and knowledge."

Which leads to the issue of work ethic? Work ethic has to be taught. If Gen Yers didn't learn it at home — like most Boomers did — or at another job, guess what? Their manager needs to teach them explicitly what "work ethic" means in their organization. And, don't think you're role modeling it because you put in 60 to 70 hours a week! That's not work ethic to young people; that's insanity!

Gen Y Project:

You mean managers are expected to take the time to teach work ethic?

Carolyn:

Absolutely! If work ethic in your organization means employees have to show up on time, and that's not negotiable, then make that a clear expectation, enforce it, and hold them accountable. If it means that deadlines have to met, then make that clear and hold them accountable. But remember, like Xers, Gen Yers realize there's more to life than work, and that's not a bad thing. Anna Quindlen wrote a great editorial in Newsweek last year about this very issue. She concluded: "If they [Gen Yers] prefer not to go straight from the classroom to the cubicle to the coffin, it doesn't mean they're lazy. It means they're sane."

Gen Y Project:

That's an eye-opening insight! What other Gen Y characteristics are on your list?

Carolyn:

Gen Yers are the most socially conscious generation since the 60s. Think about it. Their parents are Baby Boomers — many of whom lived through and participated in the great social movements of the 60s. Gen Yers, spurred on by community service projects in high school and college, have the highest volunteerism rate in decades.

And, they're very concerned about sustainability and global warming. Some researchers who study college students claim that these issues may well become Gen Yers' "civil rights movement."

Next, Gen Yers are family-focused. When asked who their heroes are, a majority say a parent. Their connection with family is something we haven't seen in awhile. Their older Gen X siblings were latchkey kids from divorced or dual income families left to their own devices.

Gen Yers are still a huge latchkey generation, but their parents are much more involved. You've heard about "helicopter parents" who hover over their son's or daughter's every decision? What courses should they take? What positions should they apply for? What 401-K plan should they sign up for? I don't have a problem with savvy parents offering savvy advice to young adults. My concern is with "paratrooper parents" who don't just hover; they swoop down and intervene. They're writing the resumes, going on interviews, fighting with managers about their child's less than stellar performance evaluations. That's not real caring; that's caretaking. And it not only delays maturity, but it weakens problem-solving and decision-making abilities. The managers of the world would love it if the Baby Boomers would just back off and let these young adults make their own mistakes, fight their own battles, negotiate their own terms, and learn from the process.

The last characteristic is that Gen Y is a "high expectations" generation. First of all, they expect that your organization is not merely socially conscious, but socially responsible. They're doing research on your company before they interview, and they're finding out how you respect the

environment, how you treat your employees, and how you give back to the local community.

They expect that your organization not only has a code of ethics, but also enforces it in its dealings with all its stakeholders. And they expect that your organization is a "career store." They are there to gather marketable skills, to learn more, and to gain opportunities for leadership. As lifelong learners, when that learning dries up, they're going to be looking for opportunities in other organizations.

The key to the career store is held by managers. Without a doubt, Gen Y is the highest maintenance workforce in history. They want feedback now, they want training now, they want recognition now, and they want to create the lifestyle they desire now. If managers can learn how to harness their energy and coach them effectively, these young employees have the potential to become the highest producing generation ever.

Finally, Gen Yers have high expectations of themselves. They want to make meaningful contributions right away. They want opportunities to use the knowledge, skills, and talents they have to solve problems, to innovate, and to lead.

Gen Y Project:

Aren't some of these expectations just a bit unrealistic?

Carolyn:

Getting a raise the first week or a promotion the first month or landing a position that's beyond their current skill level — those are unrealistic. But the kinds of high expectations I'm talking about are challenging organizations, managers, and coworkers to be even better than they already are. I've seen organizations whose contributions to the local community and opportunities for employee volunteerism are more attractive to Gen Yers than those who offer more money but less involvement. I've heard Gen Yers complain that their bosses don't know how to manage them, and they're so frustrated that they seek opportunities elsewhere.

Gen Y Project:

So what do they expect managers to do?

Carolyn:

They expect managers to manage! But what we've discovered over the past 10 years is that there is an "under-management epidemic" sweeping through most organizations. Most managers aren't doing their jobs.

Gen Y Project:

But what does that mean: "They expect managers to manage"?

Carolyn:

For Gen Yers, it's all about building relationships. Here's what I say to managers:

First of all, take the time to get to know each Gen Yer. Listen to them. Show them you genuinely care about their success in your organization as well as about them as individuals. Make building those relationships as much a managerial imperative as accomplishing results. Go for a walk, take them to lunch, have coffee: Gen Yers feel more comfortable in informal settings than in formal meetings.

Then, establish a coaching relationship with them. Yers want managers who are teachers who can help them grow and improve. Position yourself as a dynamic source of their learning, providing the resources, tools, and the learning goals they need to progress "just-in-time." Gen Yers learn best, as most people do, when they know they will need the knowledge or skill to succeed.

Next, be sure to treat Yers as colleagues, not as interns or youngsters. They can't stand condescending managers who yell and scream, and who are not approachable when they need their questions answered.

Be flexible enough to customize schedules, work assignments, projects, and career paths. One-size-fits-all is out; customization is in. Since some Yers are still in school, they appreciate a manager's attempts to balance work requirements with their other commitments.

Consistently provide constructive feedback. Don't wait for performance evaluations to tell Gen Yers what they're doing wrong. Do it daily. Tell them how to improve <u>today</u>. Avoid harping on the negative, accentuate the positive, and, most importantly, get them back on track immediately. Let them know when they've done a good job. Give them immediate praise, recognition, and rewards for great performance. Tie rewards and incentives to one thing only: performance. And make sure to deliver them in close proximity to the event.

Gen Y Project:

Great recommendations, but wouldn't these work for people of all generations?

Carolyn:

You got it! As I said earlier, the world has changed and so has the workplace and workforce. Managers need an approach that is more engaged, timely, and short-term. Without a doubt, it's harder to manage people today than ever before. It takes time, energy, skill, guts, and courage. That's why we keep telling organizations that one of their most important imperatives today must be developing managers who can nurture young talent.

Gen Y Project:

You've written that by 2010, there will be about a 13.7 percent decrease in the prime age workforce, those from 35 to 45 years of age. Will that create a leadership gap?

Carolyn:

Absolutely. This Gen X population forms the majority of our leadership pool for mid-level management positions — and it will shrink. Some organizations that had hiring freezes in the 90s are feeling the leadership crisis. They don't have people with 10 to 15 years of experience who are poised to be leaders. They need to find ways to offer their Gen Xers — and high potential Gen Yers — all kinds of opportunities to develop leadership skills immediately since the pool will be smaller.

Gen Y Project:

How do they do that?

Carolyn:

We're encouraging organizations to train their current managers to be leadership talent scouts and coaches. Managers are in the best position to observe who has the skills, talents, and drive needed to be a leader. They're in a position to provide training resources, facilitate networking, and look out for ad hoc opportunities to test drive a high potential employee's abilities. One of the biggest mistakes many organizations make is to throw someone into management without enough test-driving to see if they are suitable for the role and really like managing people.

Gen Y Project:

We hear a lot about the need for mentoring young people. What's your take on that?

Carolyn:

These kinds of relationships — whether formal or informal — shorten the learning curve for Gen Yers who are quick learners and get really impatient if they're told they won't be taken seriously until they've been with the company for four to five years.

Young people are saying, "Just because it took you nine years to master a profession doesn't mean it has to take us that long." Therefore, we're advising organizations to identify and train all those seasoned, experienced professionals who are willing to be coaches and mentors to the younger workforce. Then, create formal and informal mentoring partnerships where there can be a constant exchange of knowledge, experience, and skills. Gen Yers can teach the older pros about the latest technology, and the older folks can share their historical memory, context, skills, knowledge, and wisdom. Since Gen Yers always want to know why something is done a certain way, having the context explained is important.

Gen Y Project:

Carolyn, do you have any parting words of wisdom for us?

Carolyn:

I'll leave you with one of the closing lines from the movie In Good Company. Twenty-six year-old Carter Duryea has just been fired as manager of 51 year-old Dan Freeman. The humbled hotshot admits to the seasoned Baby Boomer, "No one took the time to give me a hard time before, to teach me what was worth knowing." To me, that's what Gen Yers in the workplace are entitled to: managers who have the skills, guts, and courage not to offer them empty praise, and not to let them think that just because they were great "Little Leaguers" they can automatically become great "Big Leaguers." They want managers to teach them what is worth knowing. That's why I say Gen Yers are high maintenance, but the effort may just create the highest producing generation is history.

POINTS FOR REFLECTION

When considering employment for the future, ask your employer the following questions:

 How does your organization contribute to the local community? How does it respect the environment? What is your code of ethics? What is your track record on enforcing that code?

 What management style do you have? How do you like to communicate? How do you like to be communicated with? Can I talk to your direct reports to get a feel for whether this is a good fit for me?

 What types of leadership opportunities can you offer a young person with my skills and experience?

 What opportunities do you offer for management and leadership development?

 Do you have a reverse mentoring program: one in which I can be mentored by an older professional and, in turn, I can mentor that more senior person in areas such as technology?

 What "life skills" will I be learning by becoming a part of your organization? (Examples include networking, customer service, public speaking, and executive presence.)

 How do you see my skill set strengthening your organization? How do you see me being of service to you and your company? How can I add value immediately?

If an employer cannot answer these questions in a way that resonates with you, it is probably best to continue your job search until you find an employer who can provide answers that work for you. As a young leader, you want to find an employer who is will-

ing to invest in your development and who will allow your voice to help drive the organization into the future.

ABOUT DR. CAROLYN A. MARTIN

An expert on generational diversity and performance management, **Dr. Carolyn A. Martin** is a world-class keynote speaker, author, and master trainer. With Bruce Tulgan, she co-authored of *Managing Generation Y*, *Managing the Generation Mix*, and *The Customer Service Intervention*. A RainmakerThinking Inc. principal since 2000, Carolyn has wowed audiences across North America, the UK, and Japan for the past 20 years. Her work has been featured in *US News and World Report*, *The LA Times*, *Global HR*, and *Nursing Management*. For more information, visit www.rainmakerthinking.com.

» CHAPTER 5 «

Learning Times Green Room: Susan Manning & Dan Balzer

"Younger people today know a lot more about technologies, skills, facts, and information. We can't assume that older generations who have more time on the planet have more skills and capabilities."

Among the many positive traits we've uncovered about Gen Y, we know that they are information gatherers and welcome the learning experience. With the easy access of the Internet, they are empowered more than any prior generation to feed their hunger for knowledge.

While Gen Yers thrive on the gathering, the way in which information and knowledge is presented makes a huge difference to this audience. Susan Manning and Dan Balzer are professional teachers and trainers who have taken a unique approach to information sharing.

The Learning Times Green Room evolved in response to the need to communicate in an online forum for learning. During a series of podcasts, educators and hosts — Susan and Dan — think out loud about learning in many different contexts. They conduct interviews, participate in debates, and generate casual conversations on a wide variety of learning-related topics. Individually, the two have worked in K-12, higher education, and the corporate side of learning where they are students as well as

teachers: learning how younger people work, communicate, and relate to other workers.

By using the technology that Gen Y has grown up with, the Learning Times Green Room is a comfortable space to explore this intriguing mindset. Susan and Dan regularly reach out to a youthful audience that is perfectly at home in a virtual environment. The ease with which this generation has embraced technology has fueled Gen Y's impatience with the lower levels of computer literacy they encounter in the workplace. To find harmony at work, other generations need to better understand Gen Y's values with regard to learning. Trying to mimic them will only widen the chasm since they scoff at these "posers." Let's take a look inside this secret playbook so we can level the playing field.

Gen Y Project:

When it comes to communications, the set of rules followed by Gen Y is very distinct from those that a Gen Xer or a Baby Boomer might follow. From your experience, do you think the generations are sharing these rules with each other?

Susan:

I would say that Gen Y's playbook is online and available electronically, but may not be available for you to download unless you're part of their inner circle.

Gen Y Project:

You bring up an interesting point here: Gen Y is tightly connected to its social network, but not in the traditional way of prior generations. What is the basis for their communication with friends?

Susan:

Certainly, social networking tools like Facebook. Recently the Pew Internet Group came out with the results from a study that said 55 percent of this younger generation has used these social networking tools.

Gen Y Project:

So do they connect with strangers they have never actually met and make this anonymous group their network?

Susan:

Yes, but they are becoming more cloistered about who can see their information. That's why email is shutting down and text messaging — accessing when it's convenient — is picking up. You can only text them if you know their number.

Gen Y Project:

They spend a lot of time online and talking in short bursts with text. What effect does this have on the face to face communication skills of this generation?

Dan:

We actually discussed this with the Gen Yers, and that was one area where they felt they needed to learn more. One woman in particular said she'd been dealing with a customer complaint and, very quickly, she felt like she just wanted to give up and walk away. Research suggests Gen Yers have trouble dealing with difficult people, and I think this is definitely a mentoring opportunity that they really value.

Gen Y Project:

Susan, you referred to "cloistering" to indicate that this generation is vigilant about maintaining a tight network. They want to be very independent but at the same time, they want a very tight network. Do they tend to rely more on their friends than their family?

Susan:

Well, yes. Technology has established the opportunity to create connections with people who have similar life experiences and values even if they don't live close to you.

Gen Y Project:

Community, to me, meant the people in my small town, or my family and extended family. To Gen Y, what is community?

Dan:

It really is the whole world.

Gen Y Project:

So how do they make their informal networks work so effortlessly?

Susan:

To them, it's effortless because they grew up with these tools. I would say that means this generation has a few things to teach us. The trick is to find out what they know that they can help us with.

Gen Y Project:

We know that they were born and raised using technology and that technology is a requirement. What else does this generation find to be important?

Dan:

For starters, they do not want to be given menial tasks; menial to them means teaching other people the technology. I pulled aside three "twenty-something" women the other day at the company where I work and asked them about what they were experiencing. They were being asked to train the older managers who had been there two or three years on how to use the computers. To these Gen Yers, helping out with technology is something they could do well, but not something they feel is meaningful. They want to be given responsibility to learn how to become a better manager — to learn better how the business works.

Gen Y Project:

What can we do to more effectively engage the Gen Yers in meaningful tasks, with the understanding that they're coming in as new employees and may not have the people skills that older generations bring to the table?

Susan:

You can pair their need to understand why they're being asked to do something with the need for mentoring and leadership. I don't mean in a manipulative way, but just by explaining to them that by looking at how their knowledge and skill sets fit into the bigger picture, they're opening themselves up to the mentoring relationship.

There are some experiences you need to have in order to develop yourself, round the edges, and make yourself a little wiser in the world of business; and generally, you learn those under the wing of someone who knows. That may be a way to blend those two into a meaningful relationship.

Dan:

One of the women I spoke with said, "I learned my job in three months. Now I'm bored." Because we take a lot longer to learn the technology,

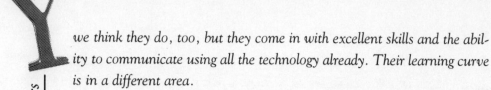

we think they do, too, but they come in with excellent skills and the ability to communicate using all the technology already. Their learning curve is in a different area.

Gen Y Project:

They have the ability to grasp certain skills with such ease. Do the older generations recognize that talent?

Dan:

No. I think in a very hierarchical environment, everyone below you on the totem pole just does what you say; there really isn't a paradigm for mutual input. You just follow orders. There's also a sense of age-ism that we perpetuate in conversations. Younger people today know a lot more about technologies, skills, facts, and information. We can't assume that older generations who have more time on the planet have more skills and capabilities.

Gen Y Project:

When it comes to Gen Y, I've found nine things that work for better communication:

1 *Listening*

2 *Being very open*

3 *Knowing and understanding their technology*

4 *Asking their advice*

5 *Being flexible*

6 *Talking to them peer to peer*

7 *Being transparent and authentic*

8 *Challenging them*

9 *Giving them the benefit of the doubt*

Out of this list, do you see any one point that is particularly effective when trying to communicate with Gen Y?

Susan:

I would go back to your sixth point — talking to them peer to peer. I think it's important to talk to the employees and get their perspective. You're only going to know if you ask.

Dan:

The first step — and the simplest one — is just to ask.

POINTS FOR REFLECTION

 As a Generation Y young adult, your knowledge and expertise can provide you with the opportunity to teach older generations about technology and world views that will affect their futures. Teaching others can provide you with a wonderful opportunity to establish a mutually beneficial mentoring relationship with Gen X, Baby Boomers, and Traditionalists.

 Learning is enhanced as you participate in team activities. As you begin to explore both career and training options, look closely at companies and educational institutions that use a highly collaborative team approach to learning and will allow you to contribute value and meaning to the learning experience.

 When considering employment, articulate clearly what you most need and want from your employer, including your desires for ongoing training and development. By better understanding your needs and wants, employers can often customize a training and development program that will support you in moving into managerial or leadership positions in the company sooner rather than later.

 Learning is not a passive process. The best way to learn is to actively participate by speaking up; engaging in rich dialogue and debate; and sharing your world views with your colleagues, professors, and bosses. As a young adult, your active participation (both verbal and written) in the classroom and in the work environment will enhance the learning for everyone involved.

Take the time to conduct a thorough inventory of everything you know and what you most want to learn. Take this list and meet with your instructor, supervisor, or boss so that you can truly focus in on what you most want and need to learn in order to be successful in both your career and life.

Note: The Learning Times Green Room draws lively conversations from its online community of educators and training professionals from around the world. Their dialogue, role explorations, reflection, and relaxation provide a behind-the-scenes, casual environment for sharing and learning. For more information, visit www.ltgreenroom.org.

ABOUT DAN BALZER

Dan Balzer designs online training programs in the corporate sector. He has also worked extensively in creating professional development workshops for college faculty and K-12 teachers on topics such as information fluency, accelerated learning, and teaching in the online environment. Dan has a bachelor's degree in history/religious studies and a master's degree in intercultural education.

ABOUT SUSAN MANNING

Susan Manning's work involves a juggling act of two very diverse groups of learners: the college and university faculty enrolled in graduate education programs and her English as a Second Language students. She holds undergraduate degrees from Truman State University and Bowling Green State University and earned a doctorate in adult and community education and higher education administration from Ball State University.

Y

» CHAPTER 6 «

Servant Leadership: Josh Sabo &
Amanda Harwood

*"If I can change one person's life, then I know I
have some worth in this world."*

G en Y represents a population of youthful, energetic people
who believe that servant leadership is the norm, not the
exception. They are actively engaged in helping others to improve
their lives. So, although they have been accused of being self-serving, Gen Yers commit a greater part of their lives to serving others
than previous generations.

With Generation Y, we have a new group of young leaders who
are passionate about affecting change in their lives and the world
around them. While they are following their entrepreneurial spirit,
they have integrated the desire to make a difference in the world
into their business plans and volunteerism into their corporate culture. These core values permeate into their decisions of what to buy
and where to work.

The Higher Education Research Institute of University of Cali-
fornia-Los Angeles recently surveyed 263,000 students at more than
385 colleges in the United States. Two-thirds of college freshmen
believe it is essential or very important to help others in difficulty.

Another survey of 13 to 25 year-olds revealed that about 81%
of them have volunteered in the last year; 69% consider a compa-

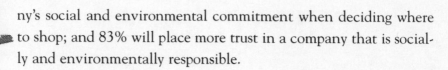

ny's social and environmental commitment when deciding where to shop; and 83% will place more trust in a company that is socially and environmentally responsible.

Gen Yers, more than any group before them, are passionate about stewardship. They embrace this concept of taking charge of something that is entrusted to them but not actually in their possession. Some indigenous cultures teach a thinking concept where you project forward seven generations to foresee the impacts of what your decisions will be. This idea is reflected in our new generation of ambitious yet caring leaders.

Where does this vision come from? Let's tale a look at nine influences that have helped to shape their mindset:

1 In their lifetime, economic prosperity has been a constant. They have few needs, and the choices they can make are abundant.

2 The visual images of terrorism and racism have flooded the media. These images share the stories of need across the world.

3 Celebrities adopt causes and concerns as a means of softening their images, which raises their cool factor in the eyes of Gen Y.

4 The world is flattening through technology, making it easier to build relationships with people in any location.

5 Volunteerism is encouraged and often a prerequisite for graduation at many high schools and, now, college. So this mentality is programmed from a very early age.

6 Experiences have become the currency of life. A new and exciting adventure that separates you from others gives you something to share with friends.

7 The survivor effect: the things that you have to do to challenge yourself are becoming more meaningful.

8 Meaning is highly engaging.

9 The gap between those who have and who have not is broadening and has created a need to earn something other than fame and fortune.

In order to better communicate with Gen Y, we need to understand their priorities. This spirit of viral volunteerism is an integral part of their being. Josh Sabo and Amanda Harwood are college students and stellar examples of servant leadership in Gen Y.

Gen Y Project:

Josh and Amanda, your experiences are inspiring. Please tell us about the volunteer work you've been involved in.

Josh:

I've spent time in New Orleans cleaning up there, and over the past few summers, my church has been taking a group of students to Camp Barnabas in Purdy, Missouri, to help special-needs kids have a week of summer camp. I've gone to a reservation at Nett Lake, Minnesota, to help run an after-school program. Beyond that, we've raised awareness for Compassion International, One Life Revolution, and some other organizations. These organizations are dedicated to helping children's causes in Africa, including poverty, AIDS, and HIV.

Amanda:

I have worked with kids at an after-school program through Youth for Christ. This year, I am leading a junior high youth group. I, too, have

worked with Camp Barnabas and I've been on two reservations, working with YouthWorks and my home church. I've also sponsored two Compassion International children.

Gen Y Project:

What was the most powerful experience you've had over the last couple of years?

Josh:

While we were cleaning up a house in New Orleans after Katrina, the owner showed up. He told us how he'd been in a car accident and wanted to see if he could salvage some trophies and things like that for his kids, but he hadn't been able to because of the accident. As we were cleaning out the house, we looked at things that were salvageable and set those aside. When the man came by the next time, he was just moved to tears. It was a big moment for me because I'd seen so much on the news that I'd become numb to it. But going down there and really seeing the devastation and getting to help was a moment that woke me up.

Amanda:

I was at Camp Barnabas two years ago. My camper was 15 and her brain function was just like any other 15 year-old, except she had cerebral palsy and another condition with her hip, so she could not move her legs or her arms.

We were sitting in the cabin one day and I have in front of me this girl who can't walk, can't brush her teeth, can't feed herself, and, for the most part, can't do anything for herself. She looked at me and said, "I look around and I see all these kids with disabilities and I feel how blessed I am." I thought that was amazing. We focus on our own problems and trivial issues while these kids who have so many challenges and obstacles to overcome are just feeling so blessed to be alive.

Gen Y Project:

Amazing! So those are some of the rewards, but what motivated you to get started with volunteering in the first place?

Josh:

For me, opportunities just came up. It sounded like something fun, something different to do — whether it was to go to a nursing home and singing Christmas carols, or working on a house. Once you do it, you realize that the joy you get from helping others is so much greater than doing something for myself.

Amanda:

If I can change one person's life, then I know I have some worth in this world.

Gen Y Project:

How have your experiences shaped you and the people around you?

Josh:

I felt like I got more out of it than I gave. It really helps to put life in perspective so you can appreciate what you have.

Amanda:

I enjoy sharing with people so I can maybe motivate them to volunteer as well.

Gen Y Project:

How about this idea of social responsibility? Companies and celebrities are jumping on board to help out with many social causes — maybe for their own good, maybe for the good of others. How do you feel about that?

Josh:

I heard you say earlier that there's a 'cool factor' attached to volunteering, and I agree 100 percent. I guess if good stuff is happening, even if somebody wants to take up the cause of Africa to make themselves look good but change is happening anyway, then I think it's a good thing.

Gen Y Project:

You're both college students. As you think about your careers, what commitments would you like to see from companies that you might want to work for or organizations that would help you continue this stewardship focus?

Josh:

Africa is a hot topic, and there are a lot of things that need to be changed over there. I think any help goes a long way. If a company said, "We're going to give three percent of our profits to build wells in Africa," then people would hear that and it would certainly attract me to really look closely at working with that company.

Amanda:

I think the commitment to honesty. If a company tells the public they are going to give 15 percent to help the hunger issue in Africa, I want to know that they are giving that 15 percent and not being dishonest about where the money is going.

Gen Y Project:

So transparency is a big issue. What do you think happens to companies that aren't transparent?

Josh:

Lack of transparency would really shut down people being involved with those organizations.

Gen Y Project:

Josh, how much do you think technology plays a part in mobilizing Gen Y for social causes?

Josh:

Invisible Children is an excellent example of how technology is really helping. It was started by three guys who went to Uganda and made a documentary. One of the issues that they wanted the government to address was the night commuting of children in Uganda. Basically, the rebel forces were abducting children and training them as soldiers. Children who wanted to avoid abduction would have to travel to safe houses outside their village. There would be hundreds of children crowded in buildings surrounded by barbed wire fences just so they wouldn't get abducted. Then they would get up at sunrise and walk several miles back to their homes.

Invisible Children used social networking sites like MySpace to organize an event called the Global Night Commute. They challenged anybody who'd seen the documentary or knew about the cause to go spend the night on the steps of a capitol building in different cities. While people were spending the night on these steps, they were writing letters to the government officials and asking them to do something. MySpace really helped get the word out about the event.

Gen Y Project:

I know it resulted in a resolution in Congress, and I think it passed in one day — which is a record in Congress. Amanda, what are some of the things the organizations do to keep you coming back or keep you wanting to be involved?

Amanda:

It's the people that are there. I worked for Campus Life last year, and there was one guy who kept asking if I was coming back, if I needed any resources, and so on. The people who manage these groups show encouragement and support. People like that, who are really passionate about the cause, motivate us to keep coming back.

Gen Y Project:

You both have certain gifts, the things you know that you do well. Does that impact what service you want to participate in?

Amanda:

It definitely does. I really enjoy high school and junior high kids and that's where I've been working for the last two years. My sister really has a passion for disabled kids and she wants to work at Camp Barnabas next summer. I've been lucky. I've had so many opportunities that fit my gifts and my passions well.

Gen Y Project:

How about after college, once you pursue your career? Do you expect to use these gifts at your job?

Amanda:

We won't be giving our best to the company if we can't use our gifts to their fullest extent. Even if it means tweaking our job a little bit, it would make that job more enjoyable. I think if a company took the time to do that, we would appreciate the company even more.

Josh:

Regardless of on what sector a company is in, I think it would benefit any employer to have employees who are less focused on themselves.

Gen Y Project:

Gen Y is deeply concerned about the future of our world. Both of you went to New Orleans. I would've never considered just picking up and moving to a disaster area when I was your age. I love hearing this generation say "I want to help."

Josh:

It's not new for us. I know some people say that Gen Y is just kind of waiting for the world to change, but there are a lot of us out there who are working to help make change happen. It's just the way we're wired, and that's exciting.

POINTS FOR REFLECTION

 By volunteering your time, talents and efforts to a social cause that needs your help, you can gain valuable life experiences while also doing something you love and making a real difference in the lives you touch.

 If you're not quite sure to begin, visit the following websites dedicated to matching volunteers with service opportunities:

- www.volunteermatch.org
- www.dosomething.org
- www.idealist.org

There are also many opportunities to volunteer abroad or get involved in work-study programs abroad that include a volunteer component. For more information, visit:

- www.volunteerabroad.com

 One of the best places to begin volunteering is in your local community by contacting libraries, animal shelters, after-

school programs, nursing homes, hospitals, and places of worship. Volunteering on a local level is just as important and necessary as volunteering for an international organization.

 One of the best ways to get involved as a volunteer is to choose a particular cause that has affected you or your family in a personal way.

 When interviewing for a job, ask your potential employer about what they do in the area of community service or foundations they have established to support people in need. If the company does not give back to the community, keep looking! Some of the best employers are those companies who give back to the community. If being of service is one of your core values, make sure that your employer values this as well. Otherwise, you may end up quite unfulfilled in your career.

ABOUT JOSH SABO

Josh Sabo is 25 and a student at Northern Seminary where he is working on a Master's of Divinity degree. He serves as a Youth Ministry Intern at Central Baptist Church in Springfield, Illinois. Josh plans to invest his life in helping young people make a positive impact on our world.

ABOUT AMANDA HARWOOD

Amanda Hardwood is 20 years old and attends Anderson University in Anderson, Indiana she is pursuing a degree in secondary education math and hopes to teach high school or junior high students within the next few years. She is currently leading a junior high youth group and serving in leadership on her college campus.

» CHAPTER 7 «

Vassar College: Andy Jennings

"Kids of today have greater understanding of the world and their place in the world. Global warming, concerns with the environment, and the political challenges we face are creating this understanding."

Vassar College has a long history of academic excellence. The name is synonymous with top-notch education. Here is an institution with standards so high that only the best need apply. And, although 90 percent of those who seek to get a Vassar education meet these stringent criteria, fewer than 30 percent are chosen.

But grade point average is not the sole measure of a Vassar student. Leadership skills are common among those who are selected to attend. As the school transitioned from being an exclusively female to a co-ed student body, Vassar College also expanded its athletic program. Here, according to Coach Andy Jennings, the true leadership of young people is exhibited.

Vassar College is an interesting microcosm of our youth. The institution perpetually attracts energetic, motivated, dedicated individuals. As a result, the culture within this community remains a testament to an exceptional sampling of up-and-coming leaders.

Now we can take a look at the Gen Y persona as a student and an athlete and see how institutions and other organizations can cultivate the strengths that might be lying just below the surface.

Gen Y Project:

Andy, athletic participation is proven to be an essential contributor to team-building and leadership development skills. As a coach, how do you teach young people to grow in this way?

Andy:

It's fundamental to what we do at Vassar. First, we all want to win and that's obviously a primary goal, but you're not going to win just by trying. We could recruit kids who don't qualify to be here in any other way in order to make ourselves successful, but that's not our approach. The process is much more important. We need to have team chemistry and to create leadership opportunities where kids are held accountable for time management and the decisions they make. There are so many different aspects in a good athletic environment, and it's the coach's role to make sure the kids develop many of these important leadership traits.

I also think this is what makes Division III (in college sports) unique. These institutions are beginning to focus on teaching individuals how to work as a team and how to become leaders. Maybe my point of view is a little skewed, but I see these athletes offering something unique in the world. Today, when everyone is focusing on the individualist behavior of young people, these men and women understand the importance of working together. I believe this is different from the athletes in Division I sports who are, in most cases, in the national spotlight.

Gen Y Project:

We're hearing about all these young twenty-somethings running companies and that they don't have the leadership skills required to be effective. Often these individuals have the academic credentials but are lacking in the extracurricular activities. Do you see this relationship between those activities and the ability to develop leadership qualities?

Andy:

Absolutely! I think that's why our college admissions process seeks out applicants who have been involved in extracurricular activities — because they have that sense of leadership.

When I was the athletic director at Vassar, I had many leaders at the college come to me and say, "We have three rowers working here in our department and they are the best workers. They're always on time, they're responsible, and they take initiative." They don't see that in every student.

Gen Y Project:

What is it about athletics that develops these qualities?

Andy:

First of all, you have young men and women clearly working towards a common goal. We basically reinforce the concept that we are all going in the right direction and need to pull together. Secondly, everyone plays a key role. Kind of like an orchestra where although each person play a different instrument, they are all important in making sure the melody is right. Thirdly, these kids go through a lot of challenges on the field. Sometimes it involves dealing with losing a game or trying to come from behind and win a game. Finally, they have to learn how to communicate with each other through verbal and non-verbal means. When you are on the field, you have to get a sense of what your teammates are going to do without always being able to ask them. You have to anticipate what they are going to do. This happens because they have spent a significant amount of time practicing together.

Gen Y Project:

What makes today's college student different from the past?

Andy:

Kids of today have a much greater global understanding than college kids did in the past. They have greater understanding of the world and their place in the world. Global warming, concerns with the environment, and the political challenges we face are creating this understanding. During the Cold War, the governments, especially ours, seemed reactive, versus today, where the current administration is taking a very proactive role. Finally, travel is so convenient today so it is easy to see firsthand what citizens from other countries think of the USA. This all produces a greater awareness.

At colleges and universities, you want to create a world where people question things because that is part of the learning process. In the television show Leave it to Beaver, *everyone had their place and defined role. Rarely did anyone question their role in the family. Today, young individuals can play many different roles, and they are encouraged to challenge established thinking.*

Gen Y Project:

How is college athletics different from the past?

Andy:

In the world of competitive sports, everything is more organized today and more competitive, and parents are into the kids playing sports. Parents "drive the bus" and make it easier for kids to play sports. They are more involved than parents were in the past, and this is true in the off-season as well as the on-season. This starts even before kids begin college. Parents view their role as part coach — making sure their kids get into the right college — and they are hugely invested in that. Parental involvement is massive. They are "helicopter parents." Do you know that term?

Gen Y Project:

No, I don't.

Andy:

A helicopter parent keeps a close eye on their child, especially when it comes to getting them into a good college and making sure they excel in college. Their behavior could be viewed as being overprotective, and sometimes they are doing this against their child's wishes.

You also have middlemen — between the parents and the coaches. This is different from recruiting services because they have individual relationships with college coaches. Kids today have their own agents to help them get into college.

Gen Y Project:

We hear so often that Gen Yers are job-hoppers after college. Do they stick with their sport while they're in college?

Andy:

To be honest, we do lose some kids during the season. It is a challenge to practice every day and still keep up with studies. However, I think athletes also learn the importance of time management and the benefits of being persistent — really sticking with something even when the going gets tough.

Gen Y Project:

In recent years, college sports have been getting a lot of bad press for behavior off the playing field. It seems to have become an increasing problem on campuses around the country. What do you think this trend says about the athletes?

Andy:

I think the press picks up on a lot of the negative news but doesn't report the positive things. I also coach the women's golf team, and so many golfers went down to New Orleans to help after Katrina. It was organized through the National Golf Coaches Association, but you don't hear about that kind of activity. That's a shame. We don't often see the positives, but they're out there in huge amounts. We do so much community work here in the area, and the local press picks that up, but in general, there is a greater sense of focusing on the negative.

Gen Y Project:

What are some of the positive aspects of a sports program, particularly at Vassar, that are being missed by the media?

Andy:

For as many negatives that they point out, there are just as many positives: leadership, respect, responsibility, discipline.

Gen Y Project:

How can an institution be successful in steering young people to the positive side and away from the negative?

Andy:

It's important that the organization create the opportunity to help the students realize their full potential. As an athletic director, I saw dysfunctional situations either because, at the time, we didn't provide the right environment for the coach and the team to be successful — and by that, I mean to develop these positive aspects — or because we had a coach that didn't believe in the philosophy of development and pursued the win-loss concept to the point of hurting those other areas.

Gen Y Project:

Is the community involvement something that's dictated by the leadership of the school or do the students naturally gravitate in this direction?

Andy:

We're fortunate in terms of the kinds of kids we get. They have always been very focused, very articulate, and very demanding of themselves and each other.

Gen Y Project:

How do the qualities that you see in student athletes translate into their ethic after graduation?

Andy:

There is one example I like to share with incoming students. Richie Webb was a history major at Vassar. He was average academically and a very good soccer player. He went and played professional soccer in Hong Kong for a couple of years. His father's Peruvian and his mother is English. When he came back from Hong Kong, he went to Peru. He spent some time playing soccer there and saw an opportunity to take some American college students to set up a not-for-profit organization in Peru called Pro-Peru. The students spend a semester there working in a valley 28 hours south of Lima on projects like changing house stoves to something that's environmentally safe, building libraries, or creating an Internet connection in a village. They get academic credit for the work. This program has become so successful that he started anther one in Belize, then one in Mexico, and now he's looking at South Africa.

Now, Richie didn't have much of a bend towards this while he was here, but he developed as he went through our program. He got a master's

degree at Oxford recently because he was awarded a scholarship in philanthropic entrepreneurialism. He's really one of these kids who is giving back in a great way, and he's a tremendous leader.

Gen Y Project:

It's interesting that you said Richie was an average student academically, and yet was able to turn his passion into an opportunity for a scholarship to Oxford.

Andy:

He won the scholarship because he approached them, presented this program, and demonstrated the importance of using young people from America to change the lives of people in another country.

Gen Y Project:

I know that many people view competitive sports as something that can create both a positive and negative environment. At an academic institution, you're dealing not just with the student athlete but also with the parents. When these parents have an exceptional athlete, aren't they looking for a highly competitive athletic program with a winning record that also has a strong academic program that will continue to develop their child's potential in this area? How does this affect that positive environment that you're trying to maintain?

Andy:

A lot of parents are starting to realize that they need to look for the right environment for their child, not just necessarily whether this team is going to win or not.

Gen Y Project:

Vassar definitely has a unique culture. The school continues to turn out young people with tremendous leadership potential. What is it about this school that perpetuates this tradition?

Andy:

It's very much an atmosphere of independence and freethinking. I've never been involved in a situation at Vassar where people are not part of the decision-making process. We make the decisions together, and we've always made the decisions together. That teaches a large number of skills from leadership to team building to decision making.

Gen Y Project:

Do you think Vassar is unique in this respect?

Andy:

I think a lot of these small liberal arts colleges, especially the ones that are described as a little more progressive, are like Vassar in this respect.

Gen Y Project:

How can others take a lesson from Vassar in order to build strong leadership skills in their students?

Andy:

For obvious reasons, I have only talked about athletics today. That is what I know the best. I think the important lesson here is that it is important to get kids — high school and college kids — involved in extracurricular group oriented activities. What we do on the field and what we achieve on the field could be accomplished in a theatre class or in an orchestra. The only difference is that there are different physical requirements.

POINTS FOR REFLECTION

 Sports are just one type of activity where you can develop leadership skills. Find what interests you and put yourself in a situation where you interact with others.

 Chemistry among a group of individuals is important. When choosing a team or an organization to join, make sure that you sense that chemistry.

 When thinking about where to go to school (as well as where to work), challenge yourself — put yourself in an environment that will require you to think creatively and solve problems using a variety of unique approaches.

 Think about the difference between an athlete playing an individual sport versus a team sport. By participating in a team sport, you can enhance your communication and collaboration skills while using a group effort to achieve a common goal.

 As you are playing a sport or contributing to a team effort, consider how this learning experience is teaching you. Look closely both at the skills you can teach and learn from being a part of a team. You may have a very special skill that the entire team can learn from in order to grow. Don't ever take that for granted — use that skill and make it known that you can offer it to others.

ABOUT ANDY JENNINGS

When **Andy Jennings** arrived on the campus of Vassar College in 1982, he was given the task of turning the school's unsuccessful soccer program into a winning enterprise. Within a short time, he delivered two conference titles and revamped the nature of the recruiting program to seek out "scholar athletes" who could continue to enhance Vassar's reputation for overall excellence.

» PART TWO «

The Entrepreneurial Spirit

Y

» CHAPTER 8 «

Extreme Entrepreneurship Education: Michael Simmons

"I've become more realistic over the past few years, but I'm still trying to hold onto that part of me that always believes something big is possible."

One of the reasons that so many Gen Yers are successful entrepreneurs is because of their belief that they can achieve great things. They take chances, unencumbered by a fear of failure because they've been raised to have unflagging self-esteem and confidence.

Michael Simmons is an excellent example of a twenty-something entrepreneur. He started his first business at the age of 16, a Web development company, an area in which he had no knowledge or experience — just the desire to try. His start-up, Princeton Web Solutions, was named the top youth-run company in the country by *Young Biz Magazine*. He also earned the Entrepreneur of the Year Award from three national organizations.

An experienced businessman when he entered New York University, Michael and his wife, Sheena Lindahl, started another venture as juniors in college. Like so many people of their generation, Michael and Sheena believe that they are capable of achieving great things. They aren't afraid to stray into unknown territory because a part of their being thrives on the challenge of the journey.

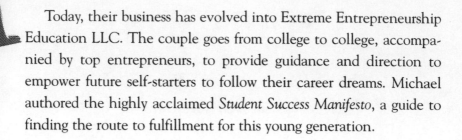

Today, their business has evolved into Extreme Entrepreneurship Education LLC. The couple goes from college to college, accompanied by top entrepreneurs, to provide guidance and direction to empower future self-starters to follow their career dreams. Michael authored the highly acclaimed *Student Success Manifesto*, a guide to finding the route to fulfillment for this young generation.

Gen Y Project:

Michael, you've already done at age 25 what most business leaders dream of doing in their entire lifetime. How did it all begin?

Michael:

I started a Web development company between my junior and senior year with my best friend at the time. We were brainstorming a lot of ideas, but realized that so many local businesses didn't have a Website and they needed one. We grew the company by outsourcing our web development for $25 an hour and charging our clients $75. We learned how to create an enterprise because we were making $50 an hour for every hour somebody else worked.

Sheena and I started Extreme Enterprise when we were juniors at NYU. I had a lot of ideas concerning business and she was paying for school herself. She started working at a venture capital firm and was working her way up. She was using an entrepreneurial mindset to do that, so we came together and brainstormed a lot of the ideas leading to Student Success Manifesto.

In our current business, we bring in some of the top entrepreneurs to college campuses for a half-day event designed to help spread the entrepreneurial mindset. We also have a website called www.journeypage.com, which is a goal support system that helps people take action on their entrepreneurial dreams or other goals.

Gen Y Project:

You talk in your book about some of the rituals to ignore — rituals that are developed in high school about what young people think is going to get them ahead in the world. Tell us more about those and how you came to understand them.

Michael:

One of the major ones is that grades in general are the main indicator of where you're going and how successful you're going to be. It might be important for many colleges and certain jobs, but I think grades are not necessarily a reflection of your learning and achievement. In the book, I was just talking about how qualities such as taking action and confronting your fears form a foundation for upgrades. And grades wear out pretty quickly after your first or second job; suddenly, it loses its importance.

Gen Y Project:

What is one thing you learned outside the classroom that has paid dividends in business?

Michael:

When you think about an iceberg, even if it looks really big, what you see is $1/8^{th}$ of the iceberg; the other $7/8^{th}$, its foundation, is actually under water. I think that's true for us as well — people focus on the assets you can easily measure and there are a lot of assets that aren't as easily measured, such as networks, branding, your health, your values, your goals, your passions. Those are really powerful.

Finding what you're passionate about, setting goals, and thinking about your values — also thinking about where you're different rather than dropping yourself into a hole you don't fit into are important too.

Gen Y Project:

So, do you see your uniqueness as a reflection of your assets, self-aware-ness, strengths, gifts, talents, and passion?

Michael:

Exactly. Most people lie on their resumes because they're applying for something that really doesn't fit, as opposed to something they're passion-ate about and then finding an organization that matches that.

Gen Y Project:

What value would you place on internships in this whole developmen-tal process?

Michael:

I think internships are really good when you find the right one, but it's not something that differentiates. I think if you're able to shadow a top-level executive at a company, you can learn more about that lifestyle and model their behavior. That can really give you good insight and it can give you incredible networking opportunities.

Gen Y Project:

But it's also important to look for and recognize the clues where your soul lights up and you're passionate about something.

Michael:

And the passion might come up in something that might not seem like a career — but you should just explore it. It may seem like a small field, but your passion will help you rise to the top.

Gen Y Project:

How do you define extreme entrepreneurism versus regular entrepreneurism?

Michael:

The traditional definition is more around starting a business and using business principles to be successful. With extreme entrepreneurship, it's the underlying mindset that the entrepreneur can use to be successful, and also a mindset that somebody can use in their job at a corporation or in their life to achieve their goals. It's all about dream and action. Instead of looking at your life and what you have, flip it and say, "I really want to accomplish this. I can get all the skills and money I need to achieve that." Then, the second thing is the action. Start and then keep on going no matter what; if you keep on going, you learn so much and you'll eventually find your niche.

Gen Y Project:

Being a successful entrepreneur is never an easy path and I'm sure you've weathered your share of storms. What advice can you offer for handling the rough spots?

Michael:

Difficult times come up because there's a lesson to be learned at some level. I personally believe that one of the best ways to learn something is to jump in and learn it experientially. I've learned the most from having the least amount of money.

Gen Y Project:

What about the temptation of the high-paying job? How do you respond to the college student that's saying "I'm going for the big salary"?

Michael:

I don't think there's anything wrong with going after a high salary, but if you're consciously giving up something you're passionate about, you are sacrificing your intangible assets. You might not realize that you're bearing those costs, but you'll notice over time.

Gen Y Project:

I think it's interesting that you started a business around web design and you didn't have that high of a skill level. You were pretty much self-taught. When you have something you're excited about and then totally immerse yourself in that topic, you can become very proficient around that skill set. I hear this all the time, 'Oh, I don't know how to do that. I can't do that.' What do you say to that?

Michael:

What's inspired me the most in that area is reading autobiographies of people that I admire. They didn't spend their whole life getting prepared; they saw an opportunity and took advantage of it.

Gen Y Project:

These are actually Boomer leaders that you're learning from. What are you learning? And what can Boomers learn from you and Sheena and other Gen Y leaders?

Michael:

I think I've become more realistic over the past few years, but I'm still trying to hold onto that part of me that always believes something big is possible.

Gen Y Project:

One of the things for our generation or the Boomers to learn is that any-thing is possible. You can put up a web page in a minute, build your business in a day, and fulfill your vision in a year. Your generation is comprised of natural networkers and the world has connected you in ways that weren't available to past generations.

Michael:

And the speed is accelerating. I was with my wife's younger sister, asking her about text messaging. It didn't make sense to me to use it because why not just use email or the cell phone? Then I realized how quickly I've fallen behind, and I'm only 25.

Gen Y Project:

That's really speaking to the transformation; you're 25 and you're learning from the 15 year-olds.

Michael:

Exactly. I've also seen some entrepreneurs doing stuff at a younger age and they think it's very common. Generally, more globally, it's showing how people even though they're younger and with very few resources can reach a worldwide audience.

Gen Y Project:

What advice would you offer to the new entrepreneur?

Michael:

Take action. No matter how daunting it may seem or challenging or unrealistic, just start small. It doesn't mean quitting your job or investing into something that's unproven, but try it out and see if it works.

POINTS FOR REFLECTION

 There are traditional entrepreneurs (who choose their activities and not their reactions) and extreme entrepreneurs (who not only choose their activities but their reactions to their activities). As the Gen Y team, we advocate becoming an extreme entrepreneur — where you are in control of your decisions and how you react to everything coming your way. This approach will allow you the opportunity to be very proactive, making positive decisions that will support you in building the most successful business and career while widening the choices you have available.

 Because of the Internet and access to technology, it is possible to open a home-based business in a matter of days with very little overhead involved. If you are someone who has a dream of opening your own business, start small, but don't wait! Act today. Contact the Small Business Administration in your area for more information on how to get up and running.

 In order to become an extreme entrepreneur, you cannot take the road most traveled. You must be willing to take risks and learn how to mitigate those risks. Taking the traditional path of earning a college degree, getting great grades, landing a prestigious internship and moving into a high paying job can serve you well, but it is not necessarily a prerequisite for success. Some of the most successful entrepreneurs in history do not hold a college degree, so don't let a lack of education stand in your way of the success you want to achieve.

 In order to become an extreme entrepreneur, leverage is the name of the game. Leverage your knowledge, good health, network, community, technology, talents and skills in order to develop the "edge" as an entrepreneur.

As an extreme entrepreneur, you will become an agent for change. This will require great courage to take a stand in the world for your passion and purpose. A mentor can help guide you through this process of transformation.

ABOUT MICHAEL SIMMONS

Michael Simmons has received Entrepreneur of the Year awards from the National Foundation for Teaching Entrepreneurship, FLEET, and the National Coalition for Empower Youth Leadership. He and his wife, Sheena, are the co-founders of Extreme Entrepreneurship Education and the authors of *The Student Success Manifesto* and *All or Nothing, Now or Never*. Recently, they were named by Business Week as one of the country's top 25 entrepreneurs under 25. As 2005 graduates of New York University, authors, teachers, speakers and award-winning entrepreneurs, they are able to deliver a unique perspective that connects with audiences. For more information, visit their website, www.extremee.org.

Y

» CHAPTER 9 «

Comcate, Inc.: Ben Casnocha

"You have to really enjoy the journey of what you're doing and not be concerned about the end result as much. That's how I try to live my life."

S uccess does not have an age. It doesn't necessarily come from years of toiling. Many successful entrepreneurs will also tell you that their success was not the direct result of brilliance.

Today's business successes come from young people who are barely into their adult years. What they lack in experience, they more than make up for with passion and guts. They recognize opportunity and seize it with both hands. These Gen Yers don't succumb to self-doubt. After all, they have been raised by empowering Baby Boomers who zealously fueled their self-esteem.

Ben Casnocha is a prime example. His "career" began in grade school when he sold pens to his classmates and gumballs to his brother because he recognized his sibling's intense sweet tooth. He identified demand and created an enterprise to meet it.

Then he made a huge leap, at the tender age of 12, when a class assignment led him to create a website that linked constituents with government officials who could answer their questions and complaints.

Ben's site was recognized by both the community and the government as a significant achievement. At 14, he founded Comcate,

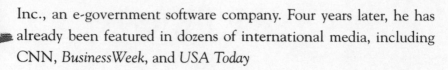

Inc., an e-government software company. Four years later, he has already been featured in dozens of international media, including CNN, *BusinessWeek*, and *USA Today*

At an age where his peers are finishing high school, Ben has already achieved more than many business people do in a lifetime. He is on the young side of Gen Y and his star is still rising. His passion, energy, and wisdom already extend far beyond his years. His commitment to social responsibility enhances his message. In Ben Casnocha, we have an exciting role model of what Gen Y can be and why those of us who are outside of this generation need to be watchful, respectful, and open to their contribution potential.

Gen Y Project:

Ben, the story of your incredible rise to success is both amazing and encouraging. Where did your entrepreneurial drive come from?

Ben:

I've always had an inclination towards identifying what wasn't working and finding a solution. I was inspired by my sixth grade technology teacher who asked us to build a Website. The class was brainstorming ideas. We were all disappointed with the uncleanliness of the seats at the San Francisco 49'ers football stadium and wanted to complain. We didn't know who to call, so I built this Website for Californians to submit their complaints about municipal issues, whether it's dirty roads or tree limbs down or potholes or code compliance issues. That site went live when I was 12.

Gen Y Project:

Did you have any experience with business or technology?

Ben:

I knew nothing, but what I think is interesting about our current time is that with the Web, no matter how young you are, you're empowered to teach yourself as much as you want. With the Web, I could research everything I wanted to know about business: how to set up a corporation, do marketing, perform customer service. Because of the Internet, I was able to do things I probably wouldn't have been able to do ten years ago. It's a democratizing force.

Gen Y Project:

The Web seems like it was a vehicle for you to achieve your goal. You identified a definite problem that fired up your passion and then sought a solution. So how did you go from the concept to the solution?

Ben:

Once that one Website went live, complaints started streaming in from angry California citizens who hadn't received an appropriate resolution to their complaint. I talked to these government authorities about my premise, trying to figure out why the complaints weren't being resolved in a timely manner. I learned that there was no technology infrastructure designed to handle incoming communications from the community.

Gen Y Project:

So here is a sixth grade student working with government officials to solve a problem that adults had just ignored. What was the result?

Ben:

My first dot-com made no money and handled maybe 100 complaints but evolved into a more successful venture, Comcate. Comcate creates software that's designed to manage and route citizen complaints, com-

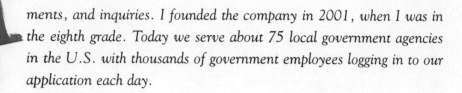

ments, and inquiries. I founded the company in 2001, when I was in the eighth grade. Today we serve about 75 local government agencies in the U.S. with thousands of government employees logging in to our application each day.

Gen Y Project:

Ben, so many people sit around waiting for the heavens to open and this huge passion to just be dropped in their laps and it doesn't always happen that way. How would you advise people who want to do something with their lives, but haven't yet found their inspiration?

Ben:

I think it's important to experiment; try a lot of different things, to expose yourself to randomness. If you travel to new places, read new books, meet new and interesting people, somewhere along the way something will "click" for you. But it takes time. Years. Decades, sometimes.

Gen Y Project:

You're measuring your success or goals by creating improvements in the world, not just the financial bottom line. How do you convey that message to other people in the Gen Y segment?

Ben:

There are a lot of drivers that motivate people to do stuff, whether it's make money, change the world, or, like Starbucks CEO Howard Schultz, to deliver health care to his employees because of a personal experience with his father. I think the most powerful driver is that of impact on other people and other organizations. Making money is not really sustainable over the long run; there has to be some other kind of intrinsic motivation. Fame or press attention is not enough; it's too extrinsic. You have to really enjoy the journey of what you're doing and not be concerned about the end result as much. That's how I try to live my life.

Gen Y Project:

How did these older leaders respond to you, knowing you were in the Gen Y age group?

Ben:

No one knows how old you are if you present yourself professionally!.

Gen Y Project:

What are the expectations of Gen Y?

Ben:

We expect broadband Internet access; we expect the ability to create and post our own work — that I'm an amateur doesn't matter — I should be able to write a blog and produce music and create a movie all on my computer. I should be able to order a book and have it at my house within 24 hours. Our expectations are totally different, but whether the people are fundamentally different, I don't know. We're just as much human as our parents.

Gen Y Project:

This generation has had tremendous advantages by all the technology that has always been an integral part of their lives. But they don't act like spoiled children. We're seeing young people who are more committed to making a difference.

Ben:

We're empowered like no other generation to do things that have meaning and can change the rules and impact people. That's why I'm really excited and extremely optimistic about what Generation Y will be able to do, not only in their own communities but for people all over the world.

Gen Y Project:

Ben, I have to keep reminding myself that you are just 18 years old. We know where you got your inspiration but how do you fuel your knowledge?

Ben:

For me, reading is the best way to learn. We all learn differently, but I love reading. If I buy one book and get one really solid original idea out of it, that's an awesome deal.

Gen Y Project:

What about mentors? Have you had the opportunity to learn from more experienced people?

Ben:

When I was starting up my business; I spent time with adult entrepreneurs, parents, teachers, coaches. I love immersing myself in an environment where people are smarter and more successful than me — I learn a ton.

Gen Y Project:

What about building a support network from the people around you? Did friends, family, co-workers, and their extended networks play a part in your learning process?

Ben:

It's important to enlist the support of the people around you. I guess we all sometimes forget these people exist and how valuable they can be. I would encourage everybody, no matter how young or old, to get those people's advice and feedback.

Gen Y Project:

Do you have some parting thoughts to share with other members of your generation?

Ben:

Some Gen Y people feel a lot of pressure from the media, society, friends — even India and China — to be successful and to make everyone happy and make a lot of money. That causes people to come up with a really specific answer to the question 'What are you going to do with your life?' Then they construct a life plan around that. I think that's a stupid thing to do. You limit your options. Sure you have a slick answer to the question, 'What are you going to do with your life?' but you miss out on all those opportunities that exist in the periphery of everyday life. So, I'm not a big long-term goal person.

Gen Y Project:

It looks like that philosophy has worked for you.

Ben:

I didn't have a grand plan around these things happening but, by staying kind of agile and open to opportunities as they sort of presented themselves, I was able to see them.

POINTS FOR REFLECTION

Ben's rich experiences as a take-charge young man can provide inspiration for people of any age who encounter obstacles. Here is some valuable advice:

⭐ Success in life occurs as a by-product of both formal studies and living the rich journey of life. Some of the best opportunities for learning exist in the periphery of your everyday life. Take time to notice and fully experience everything and every person around you.

⭐ Don't ever let anyone tell you that you are too young to start a business, live a big dream, or develop a passion project. Ben's story is proof positive that age is not a factor for success.

⭐ Comcate, Inc., was created to find a solution to a significant problem. Each time you notice a problem, ask yourself this question: "What can I do to create a solution to this problem?" You may just uncover a gold mine in the process.

⭐ Give yourself the gift of time to discover your passion and what is truly most important to you. This passion can serve as a catalyst for your future success.

⭐ Gen Y, Gen X, Baby Boomers, and Traditionalists are really not fundamentally different from one another. World events and technology have shaped their expectations, and Gen Y's expectations are simply different from those of other generations. Remember this: Every generation has different expectations, but when the day is over, all people truly want to be happy and live a meaningful life.

ABOUT BEN CASNOCHA

Ben Casnocha is the author of the bestselling book, *My Start-up Life: What a (Very) Young CEO Learned on His Journey Through Silicon Valley*. He is one of the most recognized young entrepreneurs and writers, with his work featured in the *New York Times* and on CNN. Ben speaks regularly at conferences and universities such as Duke University and the Wharton School. He is a freshman at Claremont McKenna College. For information, visit www.mystartuplife.com or his blog at http://ben.casnocha.com.

» CHAPTER 10 «

Collegeboxes: Josh Kowitt & Scott Neuberger

"Developing a business is a marathon, not a sprint."

Generation Y has demonstrated a true penchant for entrepreneurship. They're recognizing opportunities and taking action to make great things happen. What has sparked this explosion among our country's youth?

Josh Kowitt and Scott Neuberger began their journey to business success as college students. Their business, Collegeboxes, a storage and shipping solutions company, makes life easier for college students and has created a profitable business for the pair. After meeting and then graduating from Washington University in St. Louis, Missouri, the two took their idea to campuses in Boston — and ultimately, nationwide — embarking on a marathon.

Business is thriving for these two men, now in their mid-20s. But their education didn't end with a college degree. They've learned what it takes to succeed as business owners in a demanding market where customer retention doesn't exist and they need to continually replace their campus sales staff.

Their educations began in college and their business remains on campuses around the country, but the lessons they have learned have created value for thousands of people across the boundaries of business concepts, location, and generations.

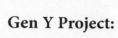

Gen Y Project:

Can you tell us a little bit about what Collegeboxes does and what it offers its customers?

Scott:

We contract with moving companies around the country and partner with them for college storage and shipping services. A moving company can't profitably serve one customer or one college — the college customer can't afford the moving services of a moving company to just move their own stuff. However, if we market to a college as a whole and get 50 or 100 — on our biggest campuses, we have over 1,000 customers — we can offer the student a good price that includes pick up, storage, and then delivery back to the room, as well as offering a profitable business for the moving company. We're middlemen in the area between the moving companies and the students.

Gen Y Project:

Great! How did you get into this business?

Josh:

I started a small refrigerator rental business at Washington University in St. Louis my freshman year and Scott started a shipping and storage company there. Our paths quickly crossed as my student employees were running into his employees in the hallways. We were delivering refrigerators and they were delivering boxes.

We merged our companies a few months later and grew quite a large business at Washington University. After that, Scott took the business model to Boston — shipping, storage, and appliance rentals — to take to other schools. He quickly started competing against a company called Collegeboxes, which was, at the time, our largest competitor. About three years ago, we acquired them, raised some money, and we've been growing the business as one company ever since.

Gen Y Project:

That's an interesting twist for such a young company. You actually bought your competitor?

Josh:

That's correct.

Gen Y Project:

Wow! Congratulations. When did you know that your company was going to be a success?

Scott:

Frankly, I was confident from the beginning that this could be what it is. I knew the business had a lot of potential when, year after year, we kept growing the customer base just at Wash U. If we could do this at 50 or 100 or 200 schools, we knew we'd really do well.

Josh:

My perspective's a little different than Scott's. While I think we have the same goals, I don't know if I ever got that same feeling, and actually, I don't know if I have that feeling today. When I started this our freshman year, our revenue was in the tens of thousands and I was shocked. On one hand, I know the value of the company, but at the same time, there's a part of me that's never satisfied, so as soon as I have achieved something I once had as a big goal to achieve, I have a new range of goals I'm aiming for.

Gen Y Project:

Let me ask you this: did everything fall into place rather easily?

Josh:

I don't think so. My parents and Scott will tell you that we're in the trenches daily with the minute details and keeping the business moving forward.

Gen Y Project:

What future plans do you have for the business?

Scott:

Our goal is to really stick with shipping and storage for college students — to go to more schools, to increase the quality of the service, and to increase how many students we service at each campus. We have actually been approached by companies who want us to start offering other services, but at the same time, our whole success to date has been based on the fact that we do one service and we do it well. We believe that our success is tied to doing one service and doing it better than any of our competitors.

Gen Y Project:

What sparked this entrepreneurial spirit?

Scott:

Going into college, I wasn't in the business school and I wasn't thinking of being an entrepreneur, but something inside of me was leaning towards it. I think starting a small side business — and then meeting Josh and seeing that a great partnership was possible — made me realize that there was something really great we could do to build a business that would meet a growing need for college students.

Josh:

When I got to college, I had a burning desire to do something in addition to academics. I wanted something to balance out my studies, and I thought starting a business seemed like a fun little hobby to do on the side. I really had no idea until Scott called me and said, "Hey Josh, do you want to get involved and come out to Boston and buy this competitor?" I said, "Sure." My hobby had gotten really big at Wash U, but it still felt like a hobby. Not until it crossed that national level did I really think about it being a business.

Gen Y Project:

How do you keep your pipeline filled? Is it from current students? Do past customers refer you, or do you have to restart your efforts to a new market each year?

Josh:

Every year is a new battle for customers. If freshmen had a good experience and the price was right, they'll use us again. The number of juniors and seniors starts to decline as the student gets older, but every year there's a new class of freshmen and a new year of marketing. Every year we go out there and market our company like it's make or break.

Gen Y Project:

What are you doing to reach that audience?

Josh:

We hire student campus managers to go out and sell the service for us. We have a really developed, fun program for them and they get paid nice commissions for what they sell. They make good money. That's the main point, especially for college students. We also work with the

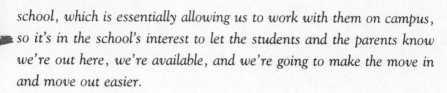

school, which is essentially allowing us to work with them on campus, so it's in the school's interest to let the students and the parents know we're out here, we're available, and we're going to make the move in and move out easier.

Unfortunately, there's no silver bullet. Every year we try to review what we did last year. What can we do better? How can we increase our customers. What can we do to get the students that are using self-storage to come to our full-service option?

Gen Y Project:

You mentioned your program for your student salespeople. You said you make it fun and pay them well. How does the training program work?

Scott:

We're trying to recruit young entrepreneurs who can execute a marketing campaign that will get more customers than anybody else, and their compensation is directly tied to that success. That's who we're looking for. They're not told to place this poster on this tree at this time. We don't say, "Here's a catalog of marketing materials that we designed and produced for a very low cost; here are some things that have happened in the past, and here is the list of all the weekly calls and reports with all the campus managers around the country and things like that."

Josh:

It really comes down to hiring the right student with the right energy level and the right mindset that wants to go for it.

Gen Y Project:

And are you finding this type of individual among the college student population?

Josh:

I think everyone wants to be successful and improve, but I see the students currently in college being even more entrepreneurial now than Scott and my friends were. Imagine if you're a college student and you see Facebook and you think, "My gosh, I should've thought of that. This guy is making a billion dollars." It lights a fire, maybe not for the right reasons, but making money does ignite something.

Gen Y Project:

You seem to have solid instincts that drove you to success. Did you have a mentor that you used to supplement your natural skills?

Josh:

Yes. We do. There are two types of mentors or advisors: the personal mentor — the person that's there when you're really overwhelmed. Then you have the other type of mentor that comes from the more business side of it. For me, my personal mentors have been my family. On the professional side, I really valued the advice of the professors we had when we were at school. Now, I really value the advice of our board members. I learn a lot about business and investment from them — stuff that I thought was way over my head, and now I'm starting to understand.

Scott:

From the very beginning, we established an advisory board, which had a couple of professors from the business school and a couple of other people that had a lot of business experience. Then, that grew into investors and a board of directors. We definitely give a lot of credit to the mentors and advisors who have helped us get where we're at today. It's very hard to do this all by yourself, and I would strongly recommend anybody to reach out to other people and find the right kind of advisors and board of

director members who can do that, even if it means giving up a little bit of equity or compensating them in some way.

Gen Y Project:

Can you talk a little bit about the employees, not necessarily the campus folks you have, but the people working in your office. With a reputation for fickleness among Generation Y, how do you retain them and keep them excited about the business? We hear all the stories about Google and their private chefs. Do you have any sort of unique fun things you do within the daily work environment that keep people engaged?

Josh:

Well...we bought a new coffee machine, which was a huge hit for our employees, and a six-pack of beer on Fridays goes a long way. One of the expectations is that we do fun things like Google does and while we can't afford a private chef, we can embrace that sense of fun in other ways. Once a month, we try to do a group team-building activity. At the last one, I brought in a Nintendo Wii and we had a tournament. It also takes a lot of effort to do these things, but they go a long way. I hope our employees appreciate it, and I think they do.

Gen Y Project:

What would you consider one of the most important components to success as a business person?

Scott:

The most important thing is leading by example and working harder than everyone else. Our employees walk in and they usually see us here already, and they usually walk out and we're still here. You can't be running in and out and be on vacation all the time, regardless of the perks and stuff you're offering. Your employees have to know that you are right beside them, working as hard as they are.

Gen Y Project:

What do you see as the mindset of the Gen Y — more entrepreneurial, more employee, or more service professional?

Scott:

I would say definitely more entrepreneurial. But at the same time, being an entrepreneur is not for everybody. It's not easy to achieve success, by any means; it's hard work.

Gen Y Project:

What are some of the most demanding challenges?

Josh:

You never realize how important and how time-consuming the little things are, and how much of a difference they make — like HR issues. All the day-to-day things that, in the scheme of things, when you're writing a business plan, you don't think about. The ability to handle the details and hold the vision for your company is a point of success or failure for a lot of companies.

Gen Y Project:

How do you keep pace with all of these time-consuming demands?

Josh:

The thing I try to keep in mind is that developing a business really is a marathon, not a sprint, and regardless of how much you think you need to work 24 hours a day to make this happen, where are you going to be

103 «

in a year? Is working 24/7 sustainable over the long haul? It's more about consistency than it is…

Scott:

Immediate success.

Josh:

Thanks, Scott…Yes! I would say pick the three things you do that make the most difference and just get rid of the other stuff. For us, that was realizing we needed to get more contracts with schools and make more phone calls to schools. Once we did that, we started to see countable progress.

Scott:

I think an underlying reason why there are so many Gen Y entrepreneurs out there is that we have a built-in advantage over an older entrepreneur because we generally don't have the ties of a family and children — at least in the early days of the business — and we can put in more time than is probably healthy to get the business off the ground. An older person may have more money and more credit history, and it may be easier to get financing, but it may not be as easy to build that early growth.

Gen Y Project:

I think that the really successful business owners are the ones that don't give up, but that tenacity seems to be in contrast to the job-hopping Gen Y. Are you an exception or an example?

Josh:

Scott and I aren't rocket scientists; we just haven't quit.

POINTS FOR REFLECTION

 Before you launch your business, make sure there is a demand for the products and/or services in the marketplace. Study the market to determine what your competitors are doing, and then test your product and/or service on a small targeted group. Follow up this test with surveys, polls and questionnaires to find out exactly how the market is responding to what you are offering.

 Collegeboxes was founded by two young college students who merged two complementary businesses (a refrigerator rental business and a storage and shipping service) into one. As you are considering building a business, you don't have to go this alone. Invest time looking closely at building a partnership with someone who shares your same vision and values, and someone whose products, services and skills can both complement and strengthen your own.

 Developing a business is a marathon, not a sprint. It is a dedication to taking care of the fine details (the little things that count) of your business and being committed to long-term endurance. Josh and Scott have been in the collegiate shipping and storage business for seven years, and their secret is: "We do not quit!"

 The best way to be successful in business is to stick to your core business — the thing that you do better than any of your competitors. As you grow, you will find it tempting to want to add new products and services, which can dilute your core business and take you away from the core that is driving profitability for your business.

 Have fun! In the beginning stages of building a business, entrepreneurs often experience a state of euphoria…everything is peaches! As the day in, day out grind sets in, fatigue is likely. Stay upbeat and positive, and always look for ways to keep the business fun. Just remember: As a business owner, you have the opportunity to make a difference in the world, and if you are having fun, the opportunity to help others will increase exponentially.

ABOUT JOSH KOWITT AND SCOTT NEUBERGER

Josh Kowitt and **Scott Neuberger** are the co-founders of Collegeboxes.com. They have been hailed by media around the country, including *The Wall Street Journal, USA Today, Fortune Small Business*, and Entrepreneur.com. *Inc.* magazine named the duo among the country's top entrepreneurs under 30 in 2006. For more information about their venture, visit www.collegeboxes.com.

» CHAPTER 11 «

The PlaceFinder.com: Arel Moodie &
Bert Gervais

"There's a huge difference between a good idea
and a good opportunity."

College is no longer just a place to earn a degree. More and more college students are finding business opportunities on college campuses and starting their careers before they graduate. These Gen Y entrepreneurs are not only seizing opportunities to start an enterprise, but they are intelligently utilizing their networks to fulfill their dreams.

Arel Moodie and Bert Gervais recognized an unmet need on their campus — a reputable, informative source for locating off-campus housing — and built a business to respond to the market opportunity. Although their original vision would have led them to a different venture, they called upon the flexibility that is characteristic of their generation and switched gears to seize a better opportunity. They sought out mentors from other generations to help them supplement their education and expand the business beyond the confines of their campus at SUNY-Binghamton. As a result, The PlaceFinder.com is spreading to campuses around the country.

What does it take to become a successful business owner when you have not yet experienced the business world? At 22 and 23 years old, respectively, Bert and Arel have the answer.

Gen Y Project:

You didn't originally start out to create The PlaceFinder.com. How did it happen?

Bert:

We were actually originally working on a vending business for healthy food in the school gym. We had secured a three-bedroom apartment and, about a week later, our third roommate backed out for personal reasons. At the end of the year, it's really slim pickings when you're looking for an apartment, so we ended up staying about a month and a half after school ended just to find an apartment. If we hadn't, we weren't going to have a place to live in the fall.

We exhausted every possible option for finding off-campus housing, and we were generally dissatisfied. The classifieds were vague or non-descriptive; the resources were slim and not organized.

Arel:

It was frustrating to hear, "This is a spacious three-bedroom home," and then you go see the home and it's the size of a broom closet. We spent a lot of time going to places that, if we would have known what the place looked like, we wouldn't have wasted our time (and gas) and the landlord's time. We probably looked at 50 or so properties that didn't interest us. Our friends were saying that the same thing happened to them. We decided we wanted to be the solution to the problem.

Bert:

So we got the idea that it would be much better if there were one place to go to that had listings and pictures. We did some research and found that our fellow students didn't know where to start looking for off-campus housing. According to Forbes magazine, two out of three students will eventually move off campus; however, most students don't know where to start. That was what really created the platform for the idea.

Coming into the fall, I had obtained my real estate license, and Arel and I had both signed up for an entrepreneurship class. We were going to the class to pitch our healthy juice bar business. But we thought about it and decided we felt strongly about addressing this problem with off-campus housing. We saw that students weren't educated about tenants' rights or what was available, and that's how www.PlaceFinder.com was born. While in the class we put up a flyer by the engineering building that read something like "Want to be part of something special? Highly motivated students email us." The motivated student who responded was Matt Young. We now had our third partner and he got the beta site for The PlaceFinder.com up in one day.

Gen Y Project:

So you created a place for students to find appropriate housing, but you were also responding to a strong need to protect the rights of renters?

Arel:

Yes. Our vision with PlaceFinder.com was to build a company that would not only help students find housing, roommates, and sublets, but would also improve the quality of the experience and the overall living situation for college students. The biggest problem we noticed at Binghamton (and now other college campuses) was that there was no one, unified voice to help students stand up for themselves when it came to off-campus housing. There was not a venue or a voice for students to be able to say, "I don't want to live in a place where the roof is falling in." Our long-term objectives are to improve the quality of student housing and to give students a voice about the quality of housing they desire. By having a business like PlaceFinder.com where everything is centralized, we do that while holding landlords accountable for their actions.

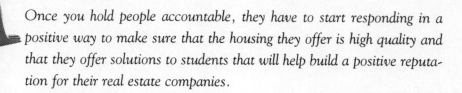

Once you hold people accountable, they have to start responding in a positive way to make sure that the housing they offer is high quality and that they offer solutions to students that will help build a positive reputation for their real estate companies.

Gen Y Project:

By holding both the landlords and the renters accountable, you're changing the whole relationship. How are you going to help more people?

Arel:

Our ultimate vision is that we want to avoid the "dump effect," which is what social networking websites were doing before Facebook. Networking sites would pull up a site and they would claim 100 schools. On the other hand, what Facebook did was really different. They made the decision to claim a few schools, get proper penetration in a few schools, and build up buzz so other schools would know about them and get students excited. They gave people an opportunity to bring Facebook to their schools and did a couple of schools at a time.

Gen Y Project:

What is your reasoning for taking this gradual approach instead of a full-fledged launch?

Arel:

We're looking to build momentum as opposed to spreading ourselves thin. We're going to be doing on-campus marketing and internships, and it's very important for the landlords to know that when they list their properties with PlaceFinder.com, they will be getting good exposure.

It's a win-win for everybody. We get to provide a service that helps people. Students get the experience of how grassroots businesses start, and they eventually get a more efficient way to find better places. Landlords get a way to decrease their vacancies and increase their profits.

Gen Y Project:

You mentioned Facebook, which is a powerful social network. At a young age, Gen Y got involved in networks they knew would help expand their entrepreneurial efforts in the future. How can someone start building a network?

Arel:

You have to put yourself out there in your community and online. When you meet someone, one thing leads to another and another. If you have this internal urge to say hello to this person, just do it. You don't know who's going to become an influence in your life. Another important thing is to actually stay in touch with the people you already know, keep them informed on what you are currently doing. You never know what could happen from that. We've all heard it's not what you know, it's who you know, but to take it a step further, it's really "who knows you". Staying connected through email, phone, online, really anyway you can is very important for this. The easiest way to do this is to build a database or a "pipeline" of contacts and what they do. Put this in one place. I recommend using ACT! or Outlook to store these.

Gen Y Project:

How do you go to school, have this business, and invest the time to keep building your network?

Bert:

Every student entrepreneur should read a book on time management or attend a seminar on time management. I read Time Management From The Inside Out *by Julie Morgenstern. Great book!*

Gen Y Project:

What did you take away from this book?

Bert:

I think that we all have this one thing we've really wanted to do for a long time, but we just can't get to it. By breaking a big project down into steps, it doesn't matter how big it is. If I just manage the little things I do, taking one step at a time, these little things will add up over time so that I reach your ultimate goal.

Gen Y Project:

What motivated you to start investing in yourself for these personal improvements versus relying solely on what you can learn in the classroom?

Arel:

In college, a lot of people focus too much on getting a degree and not getting an education; I've found that a lot of the most valuable education I've gotten has happened outside the classroom.

I've heard that all leaders are readers. If you're not taking time to develop yourself, read each day, learn from other people's mistakes, and learn time management, you're definitely not setting yourself up to go as far as you can in business or life.

Gen Y Project:

Is money a strong motivator for the Gen Y entrepreneur?

Bert:

Money is a magnifier, it just makes you more of who you already are. If you are just in it for the money, being an entrepreneur is probably not for you. Being an entrepreneur is a lifestyle dedicated to creating a unique business that helps change the world. For an entrepreneur, money is just going to pro-vide you the ability to make more choices to develop who you are.

Gen Y Project:

Where does all this wisdom come from? Did you learn your entrepre-neurial skills from your family?

Arel:

I'm the only entrepreneur in my family right now. My family is very job focused. Some of them thought I was a little crazy because when I grad-uated, I was working for a very large corporation and making more money than I've ever made in my life. I relocated, had my home paid for, had a company car — it was an amazing experience, but for me, it was-n't my own and I had to walk away from it.

It's like if you really want orange juice and someone gives you an orange drink. It may taste good, it may be almost what you want, it may quench your thirst, but it's not really what's going to make you happy. This is how I felt about working for that company. It was not exactly what I wanted, so I had to choose what I really wanted to do, which was to be an entrepreneur.

Gen Y Project:

I've heard you both mention that you have a mentor. Is your mentor older, younger, the same age, the same generation?

Bert:

My mentor is Angelo Mastrangelo a man who could be in his 60's but has more energy than people half his age, and very connected to youth. He used to be the CEO of Adirondack Beverage Company.

Gen Y Project:

What was it that impressed you enough to want him as your mentor?

Arel:

For starters, from an experience level, this guy has credibility. Second, from an integrity standpoint, he's one of the most honest people. He doesn't micromanage; he'll give you enough room to make things happen and the general guidelines and then he'll say, "You know what you need to do" or "You're missing the big picture." He's a "big picture" guy and we fill in the details. That's what helps me.

Gen Y Project:

How did you connect with him?

Arel:

When we got into entrepreneurship, we went to the owner of a local pizza place. We interviewed him about how he built his business and then asked him if he knew anyone else we could talk to. He sent us to someone else, who sent us to someone else, and we ended up back with our professor at the university, who we didn't even know owned a small business in the area. He then told us about our mentor. I interviewed him and thought, "This is the coolest guy I've ever met in my life!" Again, you don't know who knows someone who knows someone else. If we didn't talk to that one pizza shop owner, I don't know where we'd be right now. When you really want something, the universe is going to align itself so that can happen — if your heart's in it 100 percent. I really believe that.

Gen Y Project:

Some of the Baby Boomers and Traditionalists are not leading from the most creative mindset. Then these young leaders with entrepreneurial spirits — the Gen Yers — come into the workplace and the Baby Boomers and Traditionalists don't know what to do with them. How can people in today's workplace take advantage of this positive energy?

Bert:

There's so much creativity in Gen Y, and it's being suppressed. Because of that, you have these entrepreneurs breaking the mold. I read this article in Entrepreneur magazine about the "intrapreneur." It is basically someone within a company that's given the opportunity to pitch an idea, so in a sense, you're like an entrepreneur — you're seeking an opportunity. And, they are rewarded and encouraged for those ideas.

By having a culture of intrapreneurs, not inhibiting creativity, and giving some accountability, they don't feel like they're cogs in a wheel. That's a great way for the Baby Boomer generation to communicate with Gen Y.

Gen Y Project:

So, what you're saying is build an entrepreneurial culture inside a corporate culture that allows the free flow of ideas and allows Gen Yers to build projects where their creativity can explode.

Bert:

Exactly.

Gen Y Project:

We talked about what you get from your mentor. There has to be a dynamic on both sides. I've heard people say, "I don't know why a mentor would take me under his wing unless he benefited somehow." What does the mentor receive from helping a mentee?

Bert:

People love talking about an industry or topic they know about. It gets them really excited and makes it more enjoyable for the mentor. Also, believe it or not, sometimes mentors are bored. If your project is exciting, and you really believe in your product or service and you're willing to respond to the mentor's advice, there's nothing like the feeling that, "Hey, I helped someone out." The only way a mentor won't help you is if you don't ask.

Gen Y Project:

How much peer pressure are you dealing with at school, being surrounded by other people spending more time socially while you two are building this amazing enterprise?

Bert:

It's a lot of pressure. One day I was walking through a dorm, and I saw this guy bouncing up and down on a trampoline. For a split second, I wanted to be that guy because I had three million things to do and I was so stressed, but what helps me is that there's always one moment that makes it all worthwhile. You know the moment that made it all worth it for me? We have open forums on tenants' rights. This girl called me and introduced herself. She said that she had come to the forum about a week ago and had a problem with her landlord. She said she was able to get it fixed by using something in our forum. That really keeps you motivated and keeps you going.

Gen Y Project:

What advice would you offer to a prospective entrepreneur?

Arel:

Don't look for an opportunity. What you really need to do is to go about finding a problem that either you or society faces, and find a solution.

That solution then needs to be profitable and sustainable. Our mentor calls it the Opportunity Model.

Bert:

If you're an aspiring entrepreneur, you can find a list of business plan competitions at www.moot.corp.com. Pick one or two that fit your needs, and enter your business in the competition. At the very least, you get feedback from someone in your industry or with your background.

Entering competitions is really a win-win, because even if you don't win the competition, you can get valuable feedback from professionals in your industry. Most importantly, have an exit strategy. Ask yourself, if you lost everything tomorrow if your business went down how would you get back on your feet and try again? If you ask that question and answer it now, it takes away a lot of the fear in what some people call a "risky" lifestyle.

POINTS FOR REFLECTION

 One of the biggest contributions you can make to your community is to create an open forum to help solve a problem shared by the citizens of your community, college campus, or organization. By helping solve a problem, you may just land on your next big business opportunity.

 In order to build a thriving network, speak to as many people as you can. You never know who may become an influential leader in your life.

 One of the best ways to learn the secrets to business success is to interview business owners who have been successful. People love to talk about their business and their road to success, but you first have to be willing to be very curious about them and their lives.

 If you think you have a great idea for a business, start by building a simple business plan. We recommend www.OnePageBusinessPlan.com. Take this business plan to several successful business leaders and ask for their input. Then, as Arel and Bert suggest, enter a business competition through a service such as www.moot.corp.com, and see how your business idea stands up against other business ideas. This process will offer you an incredible opportunity to learn and to get ideas that will make your business idea stronger in the future.

There is a huge difference between an idea and an opportunity. An idea can be a creative spark of inspiration, but an opportunity represents your chance to solve a problem and create a profitable enterprise as a result. Look for the opportunities in life. They are everywhere!

ABOUT AREL MOODIE AND BERT GERVAIS

Arel Moodie and **Bert Gervais** are the Founders of The Place Finder LLC, a company designed to help college students find high quality, affordable, off-campus housing, roommates, and sublets. The two young entrepreneurs started the company in 2005 as students at Binghamton University when they had trouble finding suitable off-campus housing. Bert was named the East Coast Student Entrepreneur of the Year in 2006,, in 2007, The New York State Student Entrepreneur of the Year, and the Business Organization Leader of the year in 2005 at Binghamton University. Arel is a professional speaker and is well known as America's Top Young Speaker. He has spoken professionally to over 20,000 people in 8 states and two countries. They have been featured on television and newspapers such as a Fox News affiliate and in *USA Today*.

Arel likes to use his spare time to dance and has performed as an opening act for the R&B group 112. In Bert's spare time, he enjoys making music, and his band has won Binghamton University's Battle of the Bands title.

The third partner with The PlaceFinder is Matthew Young. Matthew has a background in the development of numerous technological developments, including projects used to deployed military applications. He has a black belt in numerous martial arts disciplines and is an accomplished guitarist. For more information, visit www.PlaceFinder.com.

Y

» CHAPTER 12 «

St. Cloud, Minnesota: Austin Lee & Mayor Dave Kleis

"If you don't show up, things will happen based on those who do. If you don't show up, other people will make decisions for you."

Y ou are never too young to make a difference in the world. Gen Y is a committed, responsible generation.

Traits like self-esteem, confidence, and the inability to perceive obstacles as insurmountable are of exceptional value if they can be steered in the right direction. This can happen by mentoring Gen Y and tossing ageism aside.

Fourteen year-old Austin Lee saw the need for a skateboard park in his hometown of St. Cloud, Minnesota. Rather than ask the city to build one, he presented a proposal to the mayor that illustrated how he could actively participate in making his idea a reality. Dave Kleis, mayor of St. Cloud, Minnesota and a man whose own career had a youthful start, was so impressed by Austin's maturity, wisdom, and planning that he offered him a position on the board of the city's parks and recreation department.

Gen Y is a generation of visionaries who act on their plans. They are active participants who don't let age become an obstacle to achievement. Youthfulness is not an excuse for not trying, nor does someone's age or position make them unapproachable.

At 14, Austin Lee is one of the youngest public officials serving in the United States. In spite of the fact that he had to ask his mother's permission to accept the appointment, this young man is an example of where Gen Y can be active leaders, overcome generational differences, and use their natural abilities to achieve a mission.

Gen Y Project:

Mayor Kleis, your own political career began at an early age, when you first ran for mayor at the age of 18. Can you fill us in on the start to your political career?

Mayor:

In 1989, I was a senior at St. Cloud State University when I ran for mayor. It was an experience that was quite humbling; I came in eighth out of seven candidates.

But I stayed interested and involved. I had a good friend who was then a state senator and later became lieutenant governor in Minnesota and she convinced me to take another run at office. I ran for the state senate and was elected at 29 — the youngest member ever at that time — and served for 11 years. Then I was approached again to run for the mayor of St. Cloud, did that, and won.

Gen Y Project:

So you understand what it means to be a young person with a goal?

Mayor:

You know, the world is really run by those who show up. I learned at a young age that if you don't show up, things will happen based on those who do, so if you don't show up, other people will make decisions for you. I remember a quote by Gandhi which is "Be the change you want to see in the world." I use it often. It doesn't matter what age you are; it's a matter of just participating. I always encourage young people to get involved in the change they want to see.

Gen Y Project:

So, Austin, at age 14, "showed up" with his creative ideas on how to improve the skate park in St. Cloud. What was it about him that made you want to talk to him about a position?

Mayor:

He approached me on July 4 at a celebration we had for the 150th anniversary of the city, and we talked about the need for a skate park in St. Cloud. I gave him my card and told him to set up an appointment. Austin did just that and came to the meeting extremely prepared. He had charts and graphs about a skate park that he wanted to see in the city.

When I talk to anybody who comes to the city with things that cost money, I say "These things cost dollars…" and as I said that, he interrupted me and said, "I don't want the city to build a skate park. I want to help the city build a skate park." That line impressed me greatly. I've had meetings with other folks that demand that the city do this or the city do that. He saw the need and wanted to give of his time and talent to work within the system to try and change that.

Gen Y Project:

Right from the beginning, could you see that Austin had some unique abilities?

Mayor:

Yes. He came with remarkable preparation that I don't see in people who are four times his age! And that's what impressed me. I just happened to

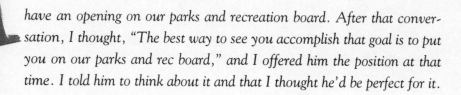

have an opening on our parks and recreation board. After that conversation, I thought, "The best way to see you accomplish that goal is to put you on our parks and rec board," and I offered him the position at that time. I told him to think about it and that I thought he'd be perfect for it.

Gen Y Project:

A very bold move.

Mayor:

And unlike other folks I've appointed to the board, he still had to go home and ask his mom!

Gen Y Project:

So, Austin, how did you became so passionate about doing something with a skate park?

Austin:

I have been skateboarding for about two and a half years. I've always liked skateboarding downtown but when my friends and I figured out it wasn't beneficial for business owners and it kind of made people mad, we just laid back on it and skated in our driveways. But we still wanted to skateboard on things like stairs, handrails and wedges — things that you'd find downtown or at universities. So, we had this idea but really didn't know how to go about it, and the opportunity came up at this celebration on July 4. That's where I'd met the mayor for the first time.

The following week, I went to his office and we talked. That's when he recommended me to the parks and recreation board. Shortly after that, the city council unanimously approved my appointment. Since then, I've been working with the city, Mayor Kleis, and everybody just trying to get things working in a positive direction.

Gen Y Project:

I understand when you went to Mayor Kleis, it was clear you had really done your homework. What motivated you to do this extra work?

Austin:

My motivation has really been to work with successful people like Mayor Kleis.

Gen Y Project:

Did you have political aspirations?

Austin:

Before this happened, I hardly knew anything about politics. Now I'm getting to know how a city really works, what the process is, and realizing that it takes a lot longer to get things done than I ever thought. I've learned a lot.

Gen Y Project:

I'm assuming you have probably a mix of generations on your council and on your park board and so forth?

Austin:

Most of them are Boomers and probably a couple of Generation X leaders.

Gen Y Project:

Mayor Kleis, what are the challenges as far as communication is concerned across the different generations represented on your boards?

Mayor:

It's usually been the lack of it. Each generation has its own way of communicating and looking at things, so it's hard for a variety of ages to reach a solution to something when you don't factor that in. I believe it's important to have a variety of views reflected in the boards and commissions you have, and in the elected offices. You have to have that multi-generational input. When you don't have that mix of generations involved in the policy-making aspect of government, you're lacking the depth of perspectives that can help a team arrive at the best solutions for the community.

In Austin's case, here's a board that deals with parks and recreation where primarily Generation Y folks or younger are using our parks. It's not that there was necessarily a conflict with the board, but there just wasn't any representation for this younger age group there.

Gen Y Project:

Tell us a little bit about what Austin has brought to your board.

Mayor:

In the last several months especially, we've had some very controversial issues to deal with. Austin does a good job of observing and really handles conflict management quite well. Often, you get people on these boards that have seen things tried that failed in the past or were being done a certain way. Once it's been done, they feel it can't be done again. Austin is coming from a fresh perspective. I've talked to other members of the board, and they see that new and fresh perspective, too. It is helping to open the board up to new possibilities for St. Cloud.

Gen Y Project:

Austin, what is the perspective you bring to the table that an older person might not bring?

Austin:

I am out there in a part of St. Cloud that the older generations don't see every day. I let them know about what's going on in parts of the city that they might miss, just because they don't spend time in those parts of the city.

Gen Y Project:

So you're going to see things that the person who doesn't go there every-day wouldn't see. That's great. Mayor Kleis, did you meet any resistance from Austin's appointment?

Mayor:

I didn't receive a lot of pushback. I make appointments based on the individual, regardless of age. I always consider, "Is that person mature enough to make decisions that affect an entire city?" My response is that Austin's more mature than some of the appointments I've made that are three times his age!

Gen Y Project:

Austin, did you get any teasing or pushback from your friends?

Austin:

Definitely no pushback. I think it's been more of a push forward. My family, my friends, and just the whole city in general have been really supportive.

Gen Y Project:

Mayor Kleis, when you're a leader — whether it's in the community, school, church, or business — what do you need to consider when choosing a younger leader to work on your team?

Mayor:

I think you need to find somebody who's engaged and wants to make a difference. That's true at any age and for any organization. I always look for somebody who has a passion and a drive and takes into consideration all perspectives. In Austin's case, we're moving forward with his project, because he has a strong work ethic. He's doing most of the legwork and fundraising, and we're going to see that his dream of working on something can happen.

Gen Y Project:

Is playing that active participant role in the process, rather than sitting back and letting someone else work on it, key to affecting change?

Mayor:

That's an age-old problem in government; there are an endless amount of folks who complain about the way things are, but very few who want to change it. If you see something you want to change, be that change.

Gen Y Project:

Austin, you had something you wanted to change and you became a part of this. What would you tell other young people about how to get started?

Austin:

Just pursue what you want to do. Let's say you want to have a role in the city. Visit a city council meeting or board meeting or just volunteer your time to the city. Keep working your way up. Just go at it with a positive attitude and do it for reasons that you believe in.

I'm having a really great experience working with the city and, as you can tell, Mayor Kleis is very cool.

Gen Y Project:

Mayor Kleis, what issues need to be addressed by older generations in order to help Gen Y become active participants in their future?

Mayor:

There are a lot of ways you can become involved, whether it's through a civic organization or just voting. The largest voting block of people is the senior citizens, and their issues are addressed 80 to 90 percent of the time. The issues of the younger generations, who vote less often, are not often addressed. If you had Generation Y folks voting in the 80 to 90 percent block, those issues — believe me — would be addressed.

Gen Y Project:

Gen Y will be the largest population by 2010, or the largest business population, which translates to voters. And yet, I read an article a couple weeks ago that said they are the lowest percentage of voters right now. How can we get more Gen Yers to vote?

Mayor:

I think it's just a matter of trying to relay to people that if you don't vote, decisions are being made by people who do. That is a huge aspect of the rights that you have; you'll decide. If you don't decide who's going to be making that decision for you, somebody else will, and you may not agree with where they're at on these issues.

There have been so many cases where things are changed just by a few votes, so a single vote does make the difference.

Gen Y Project:

Austin, from what Mayor Kleis says, you seem to be fitting in well with the other generations. What is the key to succeeding at that?

Austin:

As long as we get to know those differences between the generations, we can become the glue between the wood. It's really important we get to know each others' generations. I think that's the cool thing about St. Cloud — that they could accept a younger person to be a city official.

Gen Y Project:

If a younger generation sees that an older generation provides support, you will build that bridge of communication.

Austin:

It's like that quote, "Respect is something earned, not bought." I've seen that happen over and over in city officials, and it's been a great experience along the whole way.

POINTS FOR REFLECTION

 You are never too young to get involved in your local political community. Start by volunteering for a civic organization or sitting in on a town council meeting.

 Get to know your local officials by writing letters and introducing yourself face to face. The best way to get involved is to know the thought leaders of your community and to know where they stand on key political issues.

 Get out and vote and encourage your Generation Y colleagues to get out and vote! Because of the size of your generation, the issues that affect young people will be addressed, but only if you get out and vote!

Show up and get involved in your community, in your place of employment and in community organizations. If you don't show up, decisions will be made by the people who do, and those decisions might not be in the best interest of your community or organization.

 The best way to earn respect is to show respect to others. Get to know each generation, their perspectives and the world events that have shaped their views. Once you show them respect, they will respect you in return.

ABOUT AUSTIN LEE AND MAYOR DAVE KLEIS

Austin's story was recently highlighted on an ABC News *Person of the Week* segment, bringing attention to the positive impact this high school freshman has made on his city. Mayor Kleis, who gave up his seat in the Minnesota State Senate to run for mayor of St. Cloud, was the first challenger in 25 years to unseat the incumbent for this position.

Y

» CHAPTER 13 «

Young Urban Rebuilding Professionals: Nathan Rothstein & Ross Kanter

"If we can start changing things across socioeconomic and racial lines, we have the chance of building a large voting block that, in the future, will vote against a completely polarized way of looking at politics."

The worst of times can bring out the best in people. When Hurricane Katrina devastated the south in August 2005, the entire country rallied to provide help for the people who lost their friends, families, homes, and livelihoods.

The young people of Generation Y are well known for their desire to make a difference in the world. While many of the causes they are committed to span the globe, Katrina was closer to home and grabbed their rapt attention.

Nathan Rothstein was just about to begin his senior year at the University of Massachusetts when Katrina hit. During spring break in 2006, he went to Gulfport, Mississippi with a group of college students to lend a hand in the rebuilding process. Immediately following graduation later that spring, Nathan joined Americorps, a non-profit relief organization and spent 10 months in New Orleans. During that time, he built a network of young professionals who were united in rebuilding the city. He formed the New Orleans Young Urban Rebuilding Professionals Initiative (NOLA YURP

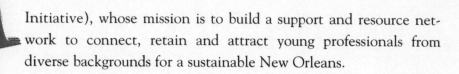

Initiative), whose mission is to build a support and resource network to connect, retain and attract young professionals from diverse backgrounds for a sustainable New Orleans.

Gen Y Project:

YURP recognizes the tremendous need for young people to rebuild New Orleans, not only in design, but in all industries — education, health care, for example. Your Website is filled with impressive stories about how young people decided to go to New Orleans and begin this effort. How did you get interested in this rebuilding effort?

Nathan:

In Mississippi, we were on the roofs every day doing repairs for different neighbors. It still looked like a bomb had gone off, and this was six months after the storm. I was shocked by what was not happening. I spoke to the people who had gone through this disaster. I asked them two questions: What money have you gotten from FEMA? Has your insurance covered anything? Most of the answers came down to "not enough."

These were American taxpayers — people who'd been paying all their lives to insurance companies and paying their taxes — and when they needed help the most, all they got were a lot of broken promises. I couldn't get it out of my mind when I went back to school. I looked for a way to come back down here, and I found out about this small organization that was working right outside the French Quarter in what was the poorest neighborhood before the storm — the average annual family income was about $16,000, and it was about 80 percent renters.

When I first got there in June, only about 50 people were living there compared to 5,000 people before the storm, so it really felt like a ghost town.

Gen Y Project:

With so much devastation, where did you begin?

Nathan:

I just started gutting homes, doing landscaping and working with different community groups. Then I began working with the urban planners who were assigned to look at how we could rebuild the city better than it was before the storm. I was able to meet a lot of people quickly and make connections. I saw a sense of real excitement that things could change, and this could be an effort that came from the bottom up.

Gen Y Project:

How did you recruit other Gen Yers?

Nathan:

About 10,000 college kids came down in March to be a part of the volunteer effort. Once I started talking to people, I found they were experiencing the same things I had seen a year before and they wanted to come back down.

I saw a need for putting up a Website that featured young people who were doing similar work and showed how people could connect. My friend, Molly Reid, wrote an article about the brain gain in New Orleans, and we quickly put up the Website. Since then, we've been receiving responses daily. Now we're looking at what we can do as a young group to make us a stronger political force in the city.

Gen Y Project:

So, you're connecting other professionals who are working on rebuilding projects in New Orleans. How do your members contribute to the cause?

Nathan:

The first people to join this network were involved in the rebuilding effort, whether as writers, planners, architects, or members of various non-profit organizations. Now we're starting to reach out to accountants or people who are studying to be doctors or lawyers.

Gen Y Project:

The Gen Yers are probably bringing in some fresh concepts around design and technology. What do you and your generation see as needs for this city?

Nathan:

There's this huge gap in education and health care that had been making the city very polarized. There was a large portion of the population that was not receiving the services they deserved.

If we can start changing things across socioeconomic and racial lines, we have the chance of building a large voting block that, in the future, will vote against a completely polarized way of looking at politics. We want things to be equal, and ideas are really coming out about how we make that happen.

Gen Y Project:

How are you connecting concerned young people with key decision-makers in New Orleans?

Nathan:

Since the city is smaller now, things are more transparent than they used to be. You have a lot of young people coming to the table with these decision-makers. Then those people talk to other young people, and there's the sense that even though you don't have much experience, now is your time to see what's possible. The people who are from here and are getting involved are well connected; they take the new people and plug them into the right networks to meet the movers and shakers and so the new people immediately make a significant impact.

Gen Y Project:

What are some of the intangible benefits that people can expect by helping others?

Nathan:

The mental health needs are so tremendous. So many people just need someone to ask how things are going. If you take the time to ask, you'll hear a story for an hour about what it was like after the storm and what it's been like trying to rebuild. Once you hear a story like that, you can't really get it out of your mind.

Gen Y Project:

These connections are building the strength of your network, aren't they?

Nathan:

It's my understanding that for the first time, a lot more organizing is going on than there was before, and a lot more connections are being made than were made before, so there are some good things that came out of the storm.

Gen Y Project:

What made you decide to stay in New Orleans?

Nathan:

I made so many connections here that I couldn't just run away. When I was thinking about what to do after college, I went back to the people I met, and they connected me to others. I started to get emails from people who were coming to New Orleans and wanted to hear stories about

what was happening. I just felt there was a need to get young people together and start organizing, to start seeing themselves as a unified base.

Gen Y Project:

What obstacles did you have to overcome?

Nathan:

Everyone is very busy and they have their own unique problems. Also, some people have more power than others do. We're connecting people to find work, and we're realizing that job-finding sites don't have the same type of personal connections we need. That's a challenge to get people into that mindset, but it's not as difficult as I thought it would be. Most people really want to get involved.

Gen Y Project:

You are pulling together a deep network with a diverse population of people from all different cultures, races, and backgrounds. How many people do you have involved in the organization right now?

Nathan:

We have over 750 members on our website, and it is growing daily.

Gen Y Project:

We're also joined by Ross Kantor, a YURP board member and a 2005 graduate of Loyola University in New Orleans. Ross, can you talk about some of the projects your leaders are working on?

Ross:

Nathan and I have been mainly focusing on getting up a master site where we can classify the various types of jobs so interested professionals can contact people within their specific field. We have people that do everything. I am a real estate developer; Nathan works with the charter school system; and our groups collectively have almost 1,000 members. At any given point in time, we can collectively message them.

Nathan:

There's a great organization called the Neighborhood Partnership Network that is working as a lead. They advocate for all the neighborhood associations and bring them together at the table to share information. Another member who was down here a couple months after the storm worked with various groups to map out the different neighborhoods and get a sense of the different territories and the major stakeholders in each area.

Some people are working for PR firms, and architects are involved in interesting projects with innovative developers that are doing exciting renovations of buildings. There's this real sense that even though we're young, we're doing things that would take five or 10 years somewhere else.

Gen Y Project:

So, it's a landscape for you to learn how to design, plan and build a city. Politically, what has to shift in order to move this city forward?

Nathan:

There needs to be more creativity brought to the table. If we're doing something in a certain way and it's not working, let's think of another way. When you bring all these young minds together, they'll provide a level of energy and creativity that will be able to solve problems in a more effective way.

Gen Y Project:

What do you see as the top problems that need to be addressed?

Nathan:

One is the lack of excellent public education. That has been a problem with the city for a while, but now there are a lot of people who are bringing their business background to the education field, and they have done some exciting work. The charter school that I'm working with is college prep for every kid, and they brought together public and private partnerships to get it going. The expectations that had been set in the public school system were so low that it didn't prepare anyone for college success. Now they're being set higher.

There needs to be a complete revamping of the mindset about what education means. You walk into the schools now and they're 100 percent segregated; they don't have the same resources as the schools in the city that are private or the public schools in the suburbs. The idea behind our school is that you set the expectations really high, and every day you tell them they can go to college, and you're changing the culture of education. We're showing how exciting it can be to learn and to advance.

Education is one of the big things that has prevented this city from having this "brain gain," where college-educated people come to the city for the first time or return here, and that's something that's changing over time.

Gen Y Project:

What else needs improvement?

Nathan:

After the storm, so many city resources lost their service and personnel. So, you have a police force that has 1,000 less officers than before, a fire department that is funded inadequately, and a health care system that has only four out of 11 hospitals open right now. There definitely needs to be improvement in all these areas, but you need money to pay city workers well. Also, a lot of people have not been given what they were promised, so there's a lack of trust that has had a negative effect on the city.

Gen Y Project:

Would you say that there's a need for inspiration or hope so that people can stop focusing on the things that aren't working and instead focus on the things that are?

Nathan:

I think unifying young people can be a real driving force in getting the city back.

Gen Y Project:

Is it possible to transform New Orleans into one of the most desirable places to live?

Ross:

Historically, New Orleans has been a great place to live. As far as the landscape after Katrina has been concerned, we have to really shake a bad image. Our congressman has been indicted; we re-elected the same mayor that let us down. I think the biggest hurdle to getting young people here is the lack of an economic stimulus to show them we have jobs, and our infrastructure is sound.

It's difficult to buy your first house with the cost of insurance and rising tax rates, and we need to shake this kind of stigma from the storm that everything is going down, and it's never going back up. I think people will

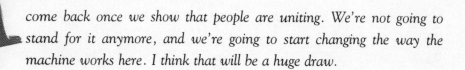

come back once we show that people are uniting. We're not going to stand for it anymore, and we're going to start changing the way the machine works here. I think that will be a huge draw.

Nathan:

Efforts are being made to market New Orleans as a great place to live, but we see that we need to take care of the people who are here right now. Then, the first time the New York Times runs the story about young people taking leadership roles, there's going to be a huge flock of people coming down, and we want to be ready for that.

Gen Y Project:

There needs to be a generational shift, and you have an opportunity to make that shift happen. How can you attract top-notch leaders to the city to support that change?

Nathan:

We are spreading the message that there are young people here who are excited about the change that they can make by working in New Orleans. If that message keeps being generated other places, more recent college graduates will start thinking of New Orleans, and the city will start appearing on their job maps. You can go to New York City or Boston and fight for scraps, or you can come down here and take a leadership role immediately.

Gen Y Project:

For a lot of people, that will be a definite attraction. How can that message be spread?

Ross:

There are smart, young people who are running for office and have credibility. They're professional and want to do something for the city that's much more helpful than the old political system.

Gen Y Project:

You've mentioned education and college students. What's the status of the universities?

Nathan:

They're coming back. Tulane has its largest incoming class ever in the fall.

Gen Y Project:

You got involved as a student. What are you doing in the area of setting up internships for college students?

Nathan:

I get a lot of postings from different places that are looking for summer interns. There's a group of 15 Duke University students who are down here working for all these different non-profits. There are graduate students from Harvard and Stanford working with small businesses to help them grow. There are a lot of people down here this summer who are doing internships. They're from all over the country, and they're falling in love with New Orleans.

Gen Y Project:

Do you have a model for expanding YURP into other cities?

Nathan:

A lot of urban professionals can help rebuild our cities; it's not just New Orleans. All our major cities are falling into disrepair. We can build this national movement around rebuilding our cities. We're going to be launching a site that will have the capability of pulling everyone together. We want to help people plug into a network and meet the type of people that will help them find what they want to be doing in life.

POINTS FOR REFLECTION

 In order to get politically involved in your local and greater community, attend Neighborhood Meetings and City Council Meetings. They are open to everyone and will give you a great sense of the residents' major concerns.

 Study your city's history, learn from the mistakes of the past, and apply this knowledge to building a great community for the future.

 If you do get involved in the political sphere, do not surround yourself with people who will **not** tell you, "you are wrong." We all need to hear straight feedback and to be held accountable; that starts with your inner circle.

 Spend time in the most under-funded, challenging public schools. This experience will provide you with the opportunity to see first-hand how we have forgotten about our poorest children, and it will motivate you to get more involved.

 Start today to build a strong network of support. There are many issues that divide people and others that unite people. Look for a group of community leaders who will align themselves in the direction of a positive shift for your community.

ABOUT NATHAN ROTHSTEIN

Nathan Rothstein graduated with an honors degree in history from the University of Massachusetts-Amherst in 2006. During college, he spent time organizing Alternative Spring Break Programs to New York City and Atlanta, volunteering for different political campaigns, and teaching in the Cambridge, Massachusetts, summer schools. He founded New Orleans (NOLA) YURP in 2007; for more information, visit www.nolayurp.com.

ABOUT ROSS KANTOR

Ross Kantor graduated from Loyola University New Orleans with a degree in Business Marketing and Finance in the fall of 2005. As a board member and a new business development specialist, je is responsible for helping to oversee the organization and planning of all the programming and economic initiatives undertaken by the organization; for more information, visit www.nolayurp.com.

» PART THREE «

The Digital Divide

» CHAPTER 14 «

Online Communities: Scott K. Wilder

"I see a place in the world for both online communities and face to face interaction. The challenge will be to motivate companies or people to use online capabilities to facilitate offline interaction."

Gen Yers are masters of technology. Their world has flattened, and the social circles have spread out farther than those of any previous generation. With texting, instant messaging, and MySpace, Gen Yers are building their social networks electronically. But while friends, knowledge, and entertainment are accessible with a click, we have to ask ourselves what they are missing by reduced personal contact.

At the same time, we have to learn how to use the technology well enough to connect with them and discover those things that we're missing but they're seeing every single day. And, surprisingly enough, there are ways that older generations can use their non-technical skills to advance the development of Gen Y.

Scott Wilder specializes in managing online communities for corporate websites. He knows the pros and cons of the 21st century social circles. As a professional who has dedicated his career to exploring technology, Scott offers valuable insight for the older generations who are still getting the hang of emailing and haven't yet tackled text messaging.

Still, there must be ways to use the power of this technology to build positive relationships. Parents, educators, and non-Gen Yers can better familiarize themselves with this vital communication tool to bridge the gap with Gen Y and to broaden their own perspectives of its potential for good.

Gen Y Project:

Scott, tell us a little bit about online communities and why they are so important to communicating with Gen Y.

Scott:

Historically, when we thought of online communities, we thought more of online discussion boards and forums. I live in Sausalito, California, where the first online community started — it was called The Well. That was just over ten years ago. Today, it's evolved from discussion boards and forums to podcasts, videocasts, and even instant messaging, which is a key form of communication among kids and teens.

I think the whole video phenomenon is just amazing. We'll see a lot more kids creating these one- or two-minute videos. I have friends, one's nine and the other is seven. They've put together a two-minute video on how to skateboard. And some of it is filmed from their phone. So, the bottom line is that Gen Y has been raised in online communities. If we want to communicate with them, we need to get up to speed on online communities so that we can build rapport with these young leaders.

Gen Y Project:

MySpace and Facebook are two of the most well known online communities. What else is out there?

Scott:

There's Teen Central, for example, which is somewhat of a help line for teens. There's eCrush.com and CyberTeens, which is a place for teens to chat. Then for those Gen Yers who are a little bit older, there are places like Lyrics.com. There are so many online communities out there. The real question becomes, I think, what area are you interested in? Once that question has been answered, then there is a good chance there is an online community that will meet your needs and interests.

Gen Y Project:

What is Gen Y hoping to get out of communicating using these social networks?

Scott:

The most basic goal is a way for Gen Y to connect with their friends. They are also used to sharing school-related information. You have students who keep their instant message window open to share ideas about papers and school projects. There's a huge collaboration effort going on for music and blogs, but these networks are used by groups of kids working together on a school project. So it's definitely communicating, networking, collaborating, and establishing a relationship with each other.

Gen Y Project:

Technology is such a natural tool for them. Is it easier for Gen Y to get online than to get in contact in person or by phone?

Scott:

Gen Yers like to email their family and instant message their friends, which I think is definitely a trend that's going on right now. It's a very powerful way of communicating. One golden nugget of information is *that a lot of Gen Y's are creating multiple instant message accounts. The reason they're doing that is because on some services, they max out at 200 names. In other words, they can't have more than 200 names in their buddy list. They're also blocking some people who are instant messaging them. This is a very powerful way for Gen Y to establish their clique or their group and to maintain privacy.*

Gen Y Project:

Do you think this channel also minimizes a feeling of isolation, even though it's a virtual connection?

Scott:

That's a really good point. I think about the issues or questions I wrestled with as a kid. One of them was, "Hey mom, can I go out and play?" And I wanted to do that to be with my friends. Well, texting and emailing are how you get around that and interact or play with your friends online.

There's the whole collaboration aspect that's really fascinating as well. Instead of "Gen Y," the term that a lot of people use is "content creators." There are a lot of ways this generation can create content together or just on their own. We've heard a lot about blogs in the last five years. Some statistics say 20 percent of teens maintain a blog where seven percent of adults do, which I think is pretty amazing.

Gen Y Project:

One thing that's really important to understand is that Gen Y is very accustomed to going out and getting instant fame and publicity by using YouTube. I think that's one thing that's a little bit different from our generation; I think we're a little bit apprehensive about putting ourselves out there on video or audio.

I think the second thing older generations fear is all the media hype about child predators. Parents say it's a little frightening to go through their kids' Facebook and MySpace accounts and start making connections in their account and see where those names lead you. I think one thing that's important to know is that MySpace and other social networking sites are being frequented by adults, age 30, 40, 45 — and there are very adult conversations that happen on MySpace. We are learning that employers are actually looking at potential employees' Facebook and MySpace accounts to see what they do after hours. I think it's important to know that once this information is out there, it is public knowledge, accessible by anyone.

Scott:

That's a great point.

Gen Y Project:

We are finding that Gen Yers are much more apt to go online than go to the library. There's so much information available at their fingertips so why should they spend time traveling when they can seek that information at home? They seem to be much more trusting of where that information comes from.

Scott:

That begs the question, what's going to happen to our public libraries?

Gen Y Project:

According to the Association of American Publishers, e-book sales were up 24 percent in 2006 and 65 percent since 2002. I'm sure this is a reflection of Gen Y's desire to use the Internet as an education resource. In what other ways is Gen Y using the Internet?

Scott:

Well, there's always that awkward time of educating kids on sex and drugs and rock and roll, so to speak, so they now have these fliers with websites where kids can go if they're too embarrassed or too hesitant to talk to their parents about sensitive issues, which I think is a good thing.

Gen Y Project:

The gaming component of online communities is tremendous. Can you provide your perspective on this?

Scott:

I look at the online gaming process as a tool to develop the whole eye-hand coordination skill set. It actually offers a great deal of both cognitive and physical learning. I believe that online gaming will become more and more collaborative as a logical thinking process — helping kids develop team skills.

Gen Y Project:

What about the growing concern of violence in these games and how it affects the players?

Scott:

I was working at KB Toys in Colorado when the Columbine incident happened. That tragedy had a huge impact on not only everybody there, but there was talk about banning kids from using online gaming because many people believed that the games promoted violence.

I think kids will find a way to access them regardless of what we try to do to stop online gaming. The question is, how do you put responsibility on the gaming companies themselves?

Gen Y Project:

I was thinking of it in the online community sense, too, where there could be 5,000 people all over the world playing this game. You have to use a lot of the same questions for parents. As parents, what are we doing to be responsible for what games our kids play and who they interact with online?

Scott:

Yes…you make a good point. There are a lot of games online that can actually teach money skills such as Monopoly online. And there are other games that are probably best to have some parental voice in. I would just encourage parents to make sure that they are clued into the games their kids are playing online and who they are interacting with online.

Gen Y Project:

I look at networking sites like Second Life and MySpace — both of which, by the way, we do use as a way to build out our network with the Gen Y Project. It's great to collaborate online and be connected to the entire world from your computer desktop, but what does it mean from a psychological perspective for the individuals who are growing up this way? Are Gen Yers finding it easier or more difficult to communicate with each other in person?

Scott:

You can't replace face to face. There has been research on everything from what parts of the brain are being activated through online interaction versus offline interaction to the risks and benefits. I see a place in the world for both online communities and face to face interaction. The challenge will be to motivate companies or people to use online capabilities to facilitate offline interaction.

155 《

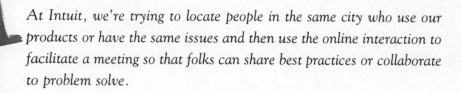

At Intuit, we're trying to locate people in the same city who use our products or have the same issues and then use the online interaction to facilitate a meeting so that folks can share best practices or collaborate to problem solve.

Gen Y Project:

You also brought up a good point about communicating behind email. Here's an opportunity for Gen Y to grow. Parents and mentors can coach Gen Y so they know when it's appropriate to use IM and when it's better to have a face to face conversation. Baby Boomers are well known for hiding behind email and voicemail, but Boomers do know how to network face to face. I think we can help by modeling how to have more face to face interactions, especially when there is a tough conversation to be had.

Scott:

The modeling aspect is really important. When I was growing up, a lot of parents would organize outdoor activities for kids. It might take a little more work on our side to get kids outside, or it might take a more structured approach where we work with kids and sign them up for activities that require face to face interaction, but I think it's worth the effort.

Gen Y Project:

Things are changing quickly. We can't continue to rely on communication tools, technology, and resources that we had back in the 90s. We've got to get brushed up on what's going on today. What do the other generations need to be doing to keep up with the times?

Scott:

It's really good to ask questions of kids, teenagers, or people in college to find out what they're doing. I think it's good to Google "Gen Y, technol-

ogy and teens" to see the trends. Rather than trying to catch up, just accept that it's evolving fast, and the best you can do is take little nuggets of knowledge as you move along and apply that knowledge to the way you operate in life.

Gen Y Project:

What about those Gen Yers that aren't getting involved with technology? How does this resistance impact their lives?

Scott:

More and more Gen Yers are going to be required to get involved because the technology's being used in the classroom. Most of the colleges today require that you bring your laptop to class and take notes that way. A lot of class lectures are on podcast now; www.oculture.com has a list of colleges and what they have in terms of podcasts.

Then you look at younger kids; as they see more kids doing it, they're going to follow the leader. The cool people in the class aren't the kids wearing leather coats or being jocks; they're the ones using technology. There's a lot of research on kids using technology that shows between sixth and seventh grade, the use almost doubles.

Gen Y Project:

Scott, another thing that fascinates me is that Gen Yers have this incredible online list of people. They are adept at building buddy lists. Is this a fad or is it going to continue?

Scott:

I think how they manage it would be the real question. But I think it's definitely going to continue. I see it even at the business level; there's a site called LinkedIn.com that is growing in popularity because it allows

hundreds of thousands of professionals to connect with each other in a manner of minutes.

Gen Y Project:

We can learn a valuable lesson from how Gen Y lives life and builds a network. You see the hesitancy of adults to dive into this. Could this be from the fear of making mistakes, as opposed to kids who just think, "I'm not going to blow the computer up" and move forward?

Scott:

Let me use the analogy of skateboarding. I recently learned how to skateboard, and I was afraid to fall where most kids are not afraid to fall. It's about being young and feeling fearless. And yes…they grew up using technology, so there is no fear around it. They just use it and figure it out.

Gen Y Project:

A colleague, Hal Macomber, who is very professional and someone who isn't going to make a lot of typos, taught a great blogging course back in the early 2000s. He said, "If you're afraid you're going to make a mistake or afraid to misspell a word, then it's not going to advance you or your blog." We have the mentality that we can't put something out there until it's perfect, but this generation goes for it and sees making a mistake as no big deal.

Scott:

There's just so much to learn, that's the best way to put it. Don't be intimidated by it all.

POINTS FOR REFLECTION

 Online communication requires proper etiquette. Don't write or say anything online that you would not want to say to someone face to face.

 In order to be successful in both business and personal communications, it is important to become adept at all forms of communication: letter writing, email communications, online messaging, blogging, telephone conversations and — last but not least — live, face to face interactions with people. We believe that a live face to face discussion is the best way to build rapport and develop trust (especially if you are a younger leader who wants to develop a relationship with a senior leader).

 By using online tools such as blogging, podcasting and vlogging (video blogs), you can convey your persona and develop rich connections with others by communicating your emotions, beliefs, and values and your stand on social and political issues.

 If you are using online communities as a way to build a network, it is important to understand that each word you write and each photograph you post can be passed around and quickly become available to anyone in the public — including future employers, athletic recruiters, and the media. If you are old enough to be building an online community, we encourage you to be responsible about what you post online. One tiny mistake online could yield huge consequences for your future.

 As a Gen Y leader, because of your familiarity with online tools (blogging, podcasting) and social networks, you have

a rich knowledge base that older leaders can tap to help them grow their business or organization. Use this knowledge, and share it willingly with your more senior leaders. They will appreciate your taking the time to share your wisdom with them.

ABOUT SCOTT K. WILDER

Scott K. Wilder is the General Manager for Intuit's Small Business Online Communities. Before joining Intuit, Scott was the Vice-President of Marketing and Product Development at KB Toys and eToys, the director of Internet services at Borders.com and Apple Computer, and has held senior management positions at American Express and Silicon Graphics. Scott worked on the following online communities: eWorld at Apple, Borders Cafe at Borders.com, and KBToys Community at KBToys.com. Scott also is a board member of the Word of Mouth Association (WOMMA) and the Society of New Communications. He received graduate degrees from Johns Hopkins University, New York University, and Georgetown University.

» CHAPTER 15 «

Zoodango.com: James Sun

"Instead of trying to figure out why each generation is different, figure out the common denominators. If we do that, we'll have a workforce that's not prideful or discriminating based on age. We will be embracing each other rather than living in conflict."

As a social network, the Internet offers a vast array of online communities. This amazing advance is also an invaluable resource when properly utilized and can bridge the gaps that exist in today's multi-generational workplace. To explore this topic, we spoke with a young man who has amassed a wealth of knowledge, business sense, and financial success by optimizing the power of the Internet and its appeal as a social connector.

James Sun, former participant on *The Apprentice* and a self-made millionaire before he graduated college, is the CEO of Zoodango.com, an online professional networking site that arranges in-person meetings at local venues.

Born in Seoul, Korea, he moved to the United States with his family when he was four with no knowledge of English. James battled discrimination and used his wits to start his first business in fifth grade. He was following the financials in the *Wall Street Journal* by the time he was 14. While going to college and working — both full-time — he managed to turn his $5,000 savings into an investment fund that grew to $2.3 million by the time he graduated.

Serendipitously, James ended up on *The Apprentice* and lasted longer than most contestants, making it to the final two. A member of Gen X, he learned some valuable lessons from Baby Boomer Donald Trump about dealing with different generations in business.

Now, at 30, James continues to build his successful life around his personal mission, "Success is having peace with yourself every day."

Gen Y Project:

I understand you and your family came from Korea to the U.S., where you faced discrimination from an early age.

James:

It was the first time in my life where I experienced discrimination, not only from a social or economic standpoint, but also from a race or diversity standpoint. It taught me a lot about what it means to endure, to ignore the naysayers, and to continue to think big. My mom always said, "Don't listen to all those people. You're going to do something great."

Gen Y Project:

And what was the first "great" business idea you had?

James:

I started my first company when I was in the fifth grade, around 11 years old. These window-cleaning guys used to go around our neighborhood, and they would get the doors slammed on them. I went to the companies and said, "Why don't you let me do it? Nobody will slam the door on me because I'm a kid!" So I got a group of friends as partners, and we signed contracts with local cleaning companies. We went door to door, got the deals, and got a cut of whatever the window cleaning service charged.

At age 13 or 14, I got interested in the Wall Street Journal and in reading about financials, companies, and how the whole market works. When I was graduating from high school, I was thinking about whether I wanted to go to college or not. I'm a huge proponent of education — don't get me wrong. All of my family has doctorate degrees, including my sister. I'm the only one who has a bachelor's, but at that time, I knew the next four years were going to be expensive — not only in terms of tuition, but also opportunity costs.

Gen Y Project:

What types of "opportunity" costs?

James:

You're giving up four years of earning potential by not being able to pursue your business. So I said, "I want to go to college, but I'm also going to start a company." I took some of my savings and started an investment fund. I was putting in about 50 to 60 hours working and going to school full-time. I was able to turn $5,000 into $2.3 million by the time I graduated college. A lot of my friends were wondering, "What is this James guy doing? He's always running in and out of class."

After college, I wanted to experience Fortune 500 company environments so I joined a consulting company called Deloitte & Touche. I got a chance to work with Boeing, DaimlerChrysler, and a couple other Fortune 500 companies and got to see what it takes to run a 10,000-employee company compared to a start-up. I also discovered my passion is to be an entrepreneur, so I left Deloitte and started a wireless software company call 3P Networks. We raised some money there, built some wireless security protocols, and sold that to a Chicago company. I then got into some other dotcom deals, helping out friends, and finally, I decided to start Zoodango.com, a social networking site for professionals, because I wanted to be involved with something that could potentially be very large.

Gen Y Project:

You've been involved in many businesses. From your experience, what do you see as the strongest trends in the business world?

James:

One of the biggest trends that I see today is social media and technology coming together. You've seen MySpace and Facebook, and there's a lot of interest right now with people trying to bridge social capital and human capital with the business world, and that's what I'm trying to achieve with Zoodango.

Gen Y Project:

Too often, the networking stops on the web, but with Zoodango, you're encouraging people to network through your site and then show up to a live event. Why did you decide to go that route?

James:

I'll start out by telling you a conversation I had with Al Erisman. He was the former Vice President of Research & Development at Boeing Company, so he had the smartest Ph.D. engineers and scientists working directly for him. When I was building Zoodango, I had an opportunity to talk with him about virtual reality and artificial intelligence. He was telling me about a project he was doing at Boeing where, if you put on a set of eyeglasses or this little headpiece, you are in your virtual world. Basically, you can put that set on and enter this virtual cafeteria, and then somebody from Boston can put on the same headset and all of a sudden, without being in the same room, it replicates the physical interaction that you're having and you're in the same cafeteria.

The computer is able to mirror the physical interaction, but when two people relate to each other, there's a lot of history. If you take two 30-year-old people, there's 30 years of history that have made up their opin-

ions, the way they look at life, and the way they act. The computer has a very difficult time mirroring the psychological and personality history of two individuals. To make it worse, you put a third person in that virtual room and the computer blows up because now you don't only have one relationship, but you have two. It's exponential. Basically, computers cannot replicate or mirror exact dynamics of human nature today. Now, ten years down the road, who knows?

Gen Y Project:

So you saw the need to do more than connect people via the computer network?

James:

We saw MySpace, Facebook, and LinkedIn — some of the bigger players — and their static approach to social networking. You can set up your profile, connect with other people, and message back and forth, but it stays online. In fact, request a face to face meeting with somebody on MySpace and you might be seen as a bit strange.

Gen Y Project:

You're working with various generations who have different communications preferences. How did you take that into consideration?

James:

We looked at how to bridge the Baby Boomers with the Gen X and Gen Y because today there's a clash in the business world. The Y Generation completely believes in a different philosophy and different work environment, and they like things that are completely different from the Baby Boomers are used to. If you talk to Baby Boomers — Donald Trump is an example — he likes to do things face to face. He doesn't like to email, he doesn't want to chat online; he wants to meet people face to face in

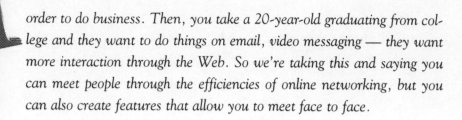

order to do business. Then, you take a 20-year-old graduating from college and they want to do things on email, video messaging — they want more interaction through the Web. So we're taking this and saying you can meet people through the efficiencies of online networking, but you can also create features that allow you to meet face to face.

Gen Y Project:

And how have you integrated the offline connection?

James:

We have 9,000 Starbucks that are integrated into our site in North America; you can see the person's favorite Starbucks to request a meeting where you say, "Look, I found your profile, I want to do business in your area and I'm looking for a partner or mentor, and I'll buy you a cup of coffee at your favorite Starbucks." Without Zoodango, you would have to try to find their email address — good luck — and if you called or got their email, they may not return your call because they're not interested in networking at this time. So, Zoodango is taking an online and offline approach to bridging the two lifestyles of the Y Generation and the Baby Boomer generation.

Gen Y Project:

You mentioned Donald Trump's preferred communication style. This whole experience of appearing on The Apprentice *must have been exciting. How did you become a contestant?*

James:

It's kind of funny how the whole thing happened. I was at the mall with my three year-old and my wife when we saw this long line of business people with three-piece suits and briefcases. I don't know if you know a lot of people from Seattle, but we typically don't dress up every day in suits; we like being a bit more casual.

We find out it's the tryouts for The Apprentice, and I'm a big fan of the show. My wife — being the great inspiration she is to my life — said that I should try out, just for fun. I said, "These guys have been waiting here since 5:30 in the morning, I don't have a resume; I'm in blue jeans and a t-shirt. I don't think I'm quite prepared." She said, "Why not just ask?" I walked up to the front and asked them if I could go in. They asked, "'Do you have a little bit of business experience?" I said, "Yeah, I've got a little bit." So I walked in. That led to about three months of the selection process — which was cool in itself.

Gen Y Project:

What was it about you that made them choose you for the show?

James:

Well, the process of getting on the show is a whole reality show in itself. I can't talk about everything, but The Apprentice is really looking for people who are mentally tough, extremely passionate, and have a certain level of intellectual ability.

First, you have to take an IQ test. Then we had to meet with a couple of psychologists; we had to take a personality test that has about 5,000 points to it. It's given by a Navy SEAL expert who understands the mental capabilities of people. Then, the last one is passion; if you don't have that, you have no chance of getting on the show. Donald Trump knows that this is one of the largest common denominators in successful people, and if you're not passionate, you come off as very boring on television.

Gen Y Project:

How would you say that translates out into the real business world when you're applying for a job or trying to start a business?

James:

It applies perfectly; if I'm looking to hire someone or find a partner, those are the three things I'm looking for.

Gen Y Project:

One of the things that was evident from your appearance on the show is your leadership ability. You showed that a leader can also step back and defer to others on the team with more knowledge or experience about a certain topic.

James:

The people on the show tend to take a one-dimensional approach to management and I've learned that doesn't work. If you get triple-A personalities on your team and you're a triple-A personality, you're not going to get the results you want if you just try to lead them around. So in the beginning, I just asked everyone to list their strengths regarding this task. I think that's one of the things you have to do as a manager; find out what strengths your team has and then give them credit.

Gen Y Project:

What else have you learned about what it takes to succeed?

James:

In college, I learned it's about what you know. When I started my career at Deloitte, I learned very quickly that it's who you know. What I also realized is that if you start after you graduate college, it's too late. While you're in college, start seeking people in the professional workplace as mentors, and for internships or references. Then, when you apply for jobs, I don't care if your GPA is 1.1 or lower; I'm hiring the student that actually started networking early. It shows proactive capabilities out in the real world. Quite honestly, you don't have to be the smartest person in the world to work in business; you have to be savvy and able to network. Every opportunity I've had has come as a result of knowing someone else. People who are professionals love to mentor and provide advice, but most people don't ask.

Gen Y Project:

That's really good advice. What is the greatest lesson you had to learn from all your experiences?

James:

I don't know if it's the greatest lesson, but it's very current and very tangible. One of the misconceptions out there is that when you want to start a business, it's going to take a ton of money and resources. I will tell you something I learned on The Apprentice. We had to do projects that, in the real world, would take two to three months, and we had to do them in two to three days. You might be saying, "That's impossible." And you know what? I honestly thought the same thing until we had to do it.

If you're forced into a situation, it's amazing what a few people can do in a small amount of time. I asked Donald Trump if he believes in really big companies, and he said there was a place for big companies, but he also believes there are a lot of inefficiencies in big companies, and he really likes to use teams that are smaller.

Gen Y Project:

James, what do you think happens when you're under this time pressure, and you know that if your team doesn't win, somebody's going to get fired?

James:

Well, first you know you can't buy any time, and you make sure every single minute is utilized. When you have three months, we all know

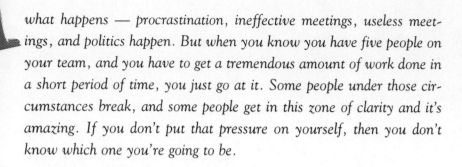

what happens — procrastination, ineffective meetings, useless meetings, and politics happen. But when you know you have five people on your team, and you have to get a tremendous amount of work done in a short period of time, you just go at it. Some people under those circumstances break, and some people get in this zone of clarity and it's amazing. If you don't put that pressure on yourself, then you don't know which one you're going to be.

Gen Y Project:

Along these lines, do you see different generations responding differently based on their individual mindsets?

James:

I'm an X Generation person; we actually grew up as latchkey kids. Both our parents were working, so we came home from school and spent a lot of time home alone. We can do things on our own. Then, we also became lonely, so now you're actually seeing where we want more community.

The Y Generation probably will be one of the greatest generations in the history of the U.S. That's not to take anything away from the Baby Boomers. Gen Y is innovative and smart, they know what's going on in the world, and the advent of the Internet has allowed them to be educated in areas that Baby Boomers and X Generation people were not. This is really changing the tide of how our world works today.

The Baby Boomers want consistency, safety, and things that are more tangible. You see a lot of different subgroups within the three and people are trying to figure out how to bridge those generations so all three can keep their identity but, at the same time, be cohesive as a society.

Gen Y Project:

Do you see an advantage of one generation over another?

James:

I don't think one generation's better than another, and I think it's going to be a fascinating time over the next five years with the Gen Y's coming into the marketplace, the Boomers still there and starting to leave the work force, and the Xers still there. There's definitely room for very creative business models. The Y Generation is going to be more well-rounded and embrace new cultures more readily because they had more access to that than we did.

Gen Y Project:

How do you get Baby Boomers to integrate new technologies into their lives?

James:

The solution is to figure out their habits, and make sure your technology is built to support but not change that habit. I've come to the conclusion that generally, people want things simple — Baby Boomers in particular — and you want to make sure you introduce a technology in conjunction with what they already do.

Gen Y Project:

As a young Gen Xer, you are somewhere in the middle in terms of how you give and get information. Can you speak a little bit about how you do your research?

James:

A lot of people ask me what financial journals I read to get my information and I say, "None of them." By the time it's in a magazine, it's too late. I did a lot of surfing on the 'Net to find the information — it's a little bit late but it's better than print publications. I'm not saying there's anything wrong with those magazines; they're very good at what

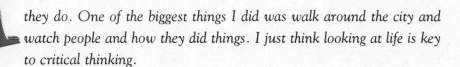

they do. One of the biggest things I did was walk around the city and watch people and how they did things. I just think looking at life is key to critical thinking.

Gen Y Project:

James, we've heard many highlights of your career, but how did you deal with the inevitable rough spots?

James:

One week, I found out three deals went sour, and I lost about half a million dollars. I remember thinking, it's very easy to just sulk, but I decided to say, "I'm glad I did." I was 24 at that time, and I had learned a valuable lesson, in that, when the market changes, your investments could change very rapidly. It's kind of cliché, but I made the experience into what I could learn from it.

Gen Y Project:

What advice do you have for Boomers, Gen X, and Gen Y for the future?

James:

I would say probably the biggest advice I have for all three groups is instead of trying to figure out why they're different, figure out the common denominators. If we do that, we'll have a workforce that's not prideful or discriminating based on age, and we will be embracing each other rather than living in conflict.

My message to anyone that's young is not to just go through high school or college passively, but to be proactive. I really believe the human mind can endure so much — it can do more than we give ourselves credit for.

POINTS FOR REFLECTION

 As a young adult entering the workforce, it is important to know that your future employers will look at more than the degree you earned or the college you attended. They are going to examine the network you have built during your lifetime. As a young adult attending college or someone who is already out in the workforce, start early building an open network, which includes a diversity of men and women from all walks of life and a variety of ages. If you enter the workforce without a strong support network, you will find it much more difficult to build a thriving career or business.

 One of the best practices for staying ahead in today's world is to get up early each morning and scan Internet news sites and industry-related blogs to get the most up-to-date news; then apply this information quickly so that you are always living on the cutting edge of business. As James said, "A lot of people ask me what financial journals I read to get my information and I say, 'None of them.' By the time it's in a magazine, it's too late."

 Each time you make a decision, and you have several options on the table, look not only at the benefits of each decision, but the opportunity costs at stake. Consider the consequences of choosing one course of action. Are you giving up another course of action whose long-term value and potential profits could be potentially greater? Instant gratification can be appealing, but be aware of its cost in terms of your success.

 There is a misconception in the business world that it takes a lot of time and money to start a business. When forced into a situation where time and resources are limited, a cohesive team can perform at a very high level of efficiency and effec-

tiveness. Don't let a shortage of time, money, and resources get in the way of building your dream business. Use your creativity and your network to work smarter, not harder.

 In order to be successful in life, find your passion and live it. If you are not passionate about your chosen career, a project, or even the home you live in, your chances of realizing true success are limited.

ABOUT JAMES SUN

The CEO, President, and founder of Zoodango.com, **James Sun** describes himself as a comedic husband to his wife and a young-at-heart father to his two kids. He loves life and lives every day with laughter and passion. James is a dynamic speaker with a unique ability to engage and captivate an audience with real life stories and industry knowledge. He graduated cum laude from the University of Washington with a Business and Computer Information Systems degree.

» CHAPTER 16 «

The Medium and the Message:
David Charles Cohen

*"I know Baby Boomers and Traditionalists love to tell
their children that they walked 40 miles in the freezing
rain to school, but that time has passed. Our world is
in a much different place today. Children are going
through other things that are just as powerful, and they
have their own incredible stories to tell. Listen and be
willing to learn from them."*

David Charles Cohen makes movies about music. His work
blends two creative media that are both designed to send a
message. His films are currently centered on well-known hip-hop
artists whose music and controversial lives are relevant to Gen Y
and somewhat perplexing to the older generations.

It's a new age and a new message. Our culture has changed. Rap
and hip-hop reflect that shift. Ballads have been replaced by stories of
life on the streets, told with raw language as foreign as the hard-fought
tales they speak of. The lyric of love has been supplanted by anger.

Not only has the music changed but the delivery of it as well.
Music is downloaded from the computer to the mp3 player.
Interestingly, though, pirating still exists, and there are plenty
within this generation that are more likely to download illegally
and then purchase it if they like it.

Every generation has its own sound and Gen Y is no different. We are in the midst of a cultural shift, both in the creation of music and movies, and in the mores behind them. David is a Gen Xer on the fringes of Gen Y and so provides wonderful insight into the changes brought by the independent film industry, the search for the next communication medium, and the impact that treating employees well has had on productivity. In this realm, David knows firsthand what the Baby Boomers can learn from Gen Y and vice versa.

Gen Y Project:

David, you started your career as a child actor in Florida doing commercials. After traveling around to New York and Los Angeles to pursue acting work, you took a break in high school but then returned to the industry by earning a degree in theatre. How did your career proceed after college?

David:

I moved out to Los Angeles again to pursue acting and quickly became frustrated with the politics of film acting. I got involved in behind-the-scenes stuff with a couple of friends and we started making some short films. From there, we got involved in production services for new, up and coming independent filmmakers that were just coming out to LA and really had no idea how to make a film but certainly had the thirst and passion to learn.

Then we opened the LA Film Lab, which was a program where we took students from an idea all the way through completion of production and took their films out to the short film market and to the festival circuit. That was extremely rewarding, but we quickly found out that the short film market was not very lucrative and it wouldn't have been much of a future if we'd stayed there.

Gen Y Project:

You've had some great life and career experiences. So tell us a little bit about the Biggie Smalls project.

David:

Peter Spirer, the director I'm working with, did a film in 1997 called <u>Rhyme and Reason</u>. It was one of the earlier documentaries that covered a huge range of rap stars — people who are huge now and were just beginning then. He had about 27 minutes of raw footage with Biggie — it was one of the last interviews Biggie did on film before he passed away, and not all of it was used for that project.

Our current documentary actually began as an investigative piece to solve the murder of Biggie, which is still, to this date, unsolved. After we got into the story, we realized it was probably in our best interests and the investors' best interest to turn it into a tribute film.

Gen Y Project:

It sounds like this film would appeal to more than one generation.

David:

Our demographic is so big; it ranges from 18 to 30 because the 25- to 30-year-olds are the people who grew up listening to him and then the 18-year-olds listen to rap and do their research and go back and listen to the forefathers, so to speak, of rap. That's what's been important in marketing to these people — we have to reach a large range.

Gen Y Project:

You fall within this age range. How does that help you to understand the desires of this segment?

David:

I was born in 1980, so I fall at the tail end of Generation Y. Growing up, I got a taste of both worlds. I saw life before the computer and before the huge telecommunications boom. I grew up with it so I was able to work with and learn it. I feel like I have an understanding of both ends of our market, which is 18 and younger and 25 to 30 year-olds.

Gen Y Project:

You're addressing a unique target market of urban, hip-hop, 18 to 30 year-old males. What do you see as the challenges in marketing to them?

David:

It's difficult because piracy and distributing content online make marketing to any generation a challenge. It's difficult to pinpoint who's going to buy — who's going to download legally or illegally. I've taken on the attitude that our movie will inevitably be pirated, but I've seen so many people download content illegally on the Internet to see if they like it, and if they do, they go out and buy it. An interesting note is that this urban demographic still does purchase DVDs at a higher rate than, say, the traditional 18 to 25 year-olds.

Gen Y Project:

But the Internet still plays a significant role in filmmaking and distribution. Correct?

David:

I feel like purchasing content over the Internet is and will continue to be the future. When we were signing our distribution contract, we had to pay attention to what used to be a very small line item on a contract:

Internet rights. I think that's going to continue to grow and one day be potentially as big a revenue generator as home video rights or television rights or possibly theatrical rights.

Gen Y Project:

What is different about this urban hip-hop market and how do marketers approach them?

David:

Because of the computer age and Internet and cell phones, it's so viral, so intensely quick. It's such a "now" generation: if it's not now, it's never. It's important to appeal instantly in that moment. So, the actual artwork on the box — the cover art, the aesthetics, the feel of it, whether it's flat or glossy — all these things play into it so heavily.

Gen Y Project:

What about the loyalty and short attention span of this audience? Are you concerned about a group of buyers who might suddenly shift to a newer trend?

David:

My generation and younger are looking at how viral and how quick things are. Instead of being upset or frustrated by the short attention span or lack of loyalty, we can actually harness it and make it work in an environment where that kind of attention span becomes productive. It might change, but for now, I believe that the short attention span is going to redefine the way work is done. But you never know; the way Gen Y works may end up being way more productive than it was before.

Gen Y Project:

This sort of shorter attention span is probably beneficial for multi-tasking, which we all have to do increasingly.

David:

I would agree. I saw a study the other day about kids that sit at their computer and do homework while they're listening to music. The parents were thinking they couldn't concentrate, but a psychologist looked at their brainwave patterns. The outcome of the study was that it didn't necessarily make them more efficient at what they were doing, but it allowed them to control more things at once while being equally efficient.

Gen Y Project:

Gen Yers want shorter bites of information so they can stop and listen, and then if they come back later, they can do it without having to miss much. Would you say that's true?

David:

Yes. As a matter of fact, if you watch MTV or VH1 or any of these channels, everything is very fast. Their shows are very short and they're cut to be able to appeal to people that just flip through the channels and capture their attention at a moment's notice.

Gen Y Project:

This fast-moving environment also includes the artists themselves. Aren't they equally fleeting?

David:

This fly-by-night pattern that's been created in the rap industry is now transcending across all forms of music. People come out of nowhere, they sell a million records, and they're making ungodly amounts of money that they've never had to deal with before.

Gen Y Project:

And how is this affecting their careers?

David:

When that money runs out, they have to fall that much farther because they haven't spent time building a solid financial foundation or network. When people who spend years building their career fall, they're surrounded by people who can help them get back up. That's not there in this industry because they didn't invest the time that I feel is important for long lasting success.

Gen Y Project:

We can't have a discussion about the music of this generation without addressing the very graphic nature of the lyrics, which cause a lot of problems for parents.

David:

Yes, that is a concern. Yet a lot of these guys are just talking about what they know or what they think is "cool." This music is based on what they know...their life and their culture.

Gen Y Project:

It's about really listening and understanding that there's a real life behind the music...a rawness about life. It's being expressed in this medium and we'd be fooling ourselves to think that this same language is not being used out there in our teen communities.

David, you've also mentioned that working with the new High Definition format is a more risky and difficult medium to market. What is the advantage of taking on this risk?

David:

When I turn on my TV, I turn on the guide and scroll through the High Def channels first. I would rather watch something in HD. To stay on top of that, it's almost another marketing point to say we can put this out on HD. It's such a new medium and people are willing to pay a premium for it, so why not go after that part of the market? At the same time, you've got to be willing to adapt if you want to stay on the top of your game.

Gen Y Project:

So how do you think viral video will affect your movie?

David:

We've licensed some film that's footage of the rapper Biggie back in the day in '93, freestyling on the street. Somebody recorded that on their video camera and posted it on YouTube.

We've been faced with the challenge of trying to remove that content because anything that we say is "exclusive," once it gets out on the Internet, is no longer exclusive, especially when it's free. We have had to deal with figuring out how to remove stuff that's out there and how to protect ourselves.

Gen Y Project:

I want to ask you about the creative film environment. Have you noticed a change among the Gen Yers entering this workplace?

David:

It's a changing environment, where you can bring your animal to work, you can play music and work, you can talk to the guy right next door, and you have these fun work environments. This up and coming generation is creating that environment, where you feel free to create, which is very different from the traditional corporate environment.

Gen Y Project:

Yes, it is definitely changing. I was talking to someone who said, "Well, I'm not sure that we can change to meet Gen Y's needs." I said, "Don't worry, they're going to change it for you."

David:

Or you'll lose the employee. They'll go elsewhere to a company that's adapting to this change.

Gen Y Project:

If you had one snippet of wisdom to give Gen Y, what would that be?

David:

I would tell them to pay attention to what's happened. Pay attention to why things are the way they are because when you become my age, it's going to help you continue to forecast what's going to happen in the future.

Gen Y Project:

And what about for the older generations?

David:

I would say, pay attention to the younger generation. Don't write them off. Be willing to adapt and change and be willing to listen. I know Baby

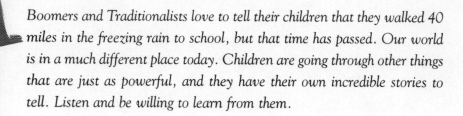

Boomers and Traditionalists love to tell their children that they walked 40 miles in the freezing rain to school, but that time has passed. Our world is in a much different place today. Children are going through other things that are just as powerful, and they have their own incredible stories to tell. Listen and be willing to learn from them.

POINTS FOR REFLECTION

 Every invention, new business or creative work of art starts with a dream, goal or desire. Give yourself time to explore. Set aside time each day to think, play and dream about what you most want for your life, and write these ideas in a journal.

 Art is a personal expression that tells a story. Before you judge something like rap, hip-hop or another person, take the time to understand the culture and story behind the person or the process.

 Rising to the top quickly or hopping from job to job can be very seductive and can seem like a "great ride." However, there is something powerful to be said for investing time around building a solid network of support and a strong financial foundation. If you are looking for instant success or you are riding the coattails of people who don't belong to a strong support system, your career may be volatile and short-lived.

 Instant access to information is creating problems with both plagiarism and piracy. Access isn't the same as permission. Before you download something illegally or copy another person's work, think twice.

A short attention span might be misinterpreted as the ability to handle more tasks than others judge possible. Turn this energy into productivity, and you can enjoy a wider range of experiences and rewards.

ABOUT DAVID CHARLES COHEN

Award-winning producer **David Charles Cohen** knows the world of film and TV both behind and in front of the camera. After 14 years in front of the camera, he founded 1421 Productions and LA Film Lab Entertainment, where he produced over 17 shorts and features. Most recently, he produced <u>Notorious BIG, Bigger than Life</u>, a documentary about the life of deceased rap artist Notorious B.I.G. with Academy and Emmy Award nominated director Peter Spirer. For more information, visit <u>www.biggiethemovie.com</u>. David is also the Chief Executive Maestro of Writers of the Round Table Inc.. For more information, visit <u>http://writersoftheroundtable.com</u>.

» CHAPTER 17 «

Live Experience Design: Kent Corbell

"Gen Y has the freedom to know that they can work smarter and not harder. They want to work mentally and not physically."

Gen Yers are presented with far more options than the older generations. As a result, they have more choices. We've learned that they will choose a location and then find a job. They reach out to a broad spectrum of anonymous people to build their social network, and yet they are fiercely protective of their inner circles. And their loyalty is short-lived in the workplace. They don't fear change, and they're open to new ideas.

With more opportunities to consider — and powered by strong commitment to lifestyle over career — Gen Y demands more than just good products and services, they expect great experiences everywhere from the store to the show.

This generational shift has allowed Kent Corbell to turn his natural passions into a thriving business. From programming his parents VCR to producing concerts in college, Kent has built his career by creating entertaining experiences. The principal of Live Experience Design, an experience creation company, Kent creates at the intersection of technology, entertainment, and communications. He has helped to develop over $70 million in groundbreaking experiences, including the fountains at the Bellagio, Cirque du Soleil's O, and fire cannons shooting flames 100 feet into the air at Burning Man.

Kent is also a member of Gen Y. He understands — and relates to — their desire for meaningful fun and their willingness to invest their time and money in quality entertainment. He sees how Gen Y affects, and is affected by, these engaging experiences. Kent also offers a visionary perspective on ways in which Gen Y will influence the world around them in a positive manner and on how we can take a lesson from their unique traits.

Gen Y Project:

Kent, what you are doing with the live experiential presentations you are creating is right up the alley of Gen Y. They want 'the experience' and they want to be wowed. We are talking about how Gen Y is flocking to interactive theatrical presentations in droves. They don't mind paying the $100 to $200 for admission tickets because they walk away with an experience.

Will you fill us in a little bit more about your background and about how you came to be so attracted to these experiential activities?

Kent:

I've always played with technology and been drawn — literally, like a moth to a flame — to crazy, involving experiences. In elementary school, I was the kid who ran the projector for teachers, and that continued in junior high, high school, and through college. When I was in junior high, I was really attracted to concerts — big gatherings of people having fun. I would just show up to a concert and jump in with the roadies and start setting things up. I had no idea what I was doing; I was just interested and wanted to learn more.

Then, over several years, after learning through trial and error and after having a lot of people give me the opportunity to come and play, I started to create extraordinary experiences. I've produced large con-

certs of every music style, and toured with several bands. I have designed and created the lighting, the sets, the sound and video, and nearly everything that comes together to create an experience that people will enjoy for a few hours, or even for a few days. What I've always loved about these experiential presentations — even more than the creation — is the impact they have on people.

Sitting on the side of the stage and watching people having a blast and being totally enthralled with the experience of the band and the music and the lights and everything is great! I've always been interested in the technology that makes it possible, but I am equally intrigued by how people respond to it.

Gen Y Project:

So, you have really immersed yourself in the industry and learned hands-on how to do what you're doing. How has the entertainment experience changed in the last two decades?

Kent:

In the past, when people attended a live event such as a concert or theatrical presentation, they went with an expectation of just sitting and watching. Today, the audience wants to participate and possibly influence what's happening around them; they definitely want to have a choice about what they're experiencing. This is particularly true for Gen Y because they've grown up being able to interact both live and online. They know they can influence what is going on in their world.

Gen Y Project:

I've noticed that this generation won't tolerate something that's not exciting or interesting. Authenticity is also key to the experience. Would you agree?

Kent:

Yes. And it's not only about being authentic — it must be something they can relate to in their life and that has meaning. Like all people, Gen Y likes to get lost in an illusion. But they also expect to personally get something meaningful out of it. It's not enough to simply be distracted for a few hours.

Gen Y Project:

Are you feeling this is strictly Gen Y or is this something our whole culture is favoring?

Kent:

I think it's where all people are moving. Gen Y, in some ways, is unique because of all the technological and social changes that are converging right now. Gen Y is more open to sharing their emotions and connecting openly. They give other generations permission to take that risk and to try something new.

Gen Y Project:

I also think businesses that are targeting Generation Y understand that they have to learn how to use these interactive tools if they want to attract the younger audience. It's Gen Y's trend to job-hop and even move from city to city, so you have to keep things exciting or you'll lose them. We believe that people have to understand that Gen Y's working habits and patterns might not fit the traditional modes to which Baby Boomers are accustomed.

Kent:

Yes, to attract and retain them, any experience has to be personally valuable to them. This goes for jobs and places to live, as well as entertainment.

Gen Y Project:

Gen Y clearly thrives on variety, and they are more adaptive to the changes that are going on in society. Why do you think change is so easy for them?

Kent:

I'm going to give you my 50,000 foot perspective on this. Gen Y is the result of thousands of years of human evolution. In the past, people's experiences were the result of their immediate family and the village where they grew up. Then, our ability to travel and experience other cultures greatly expanded. We can now move around the world very fast. Today, with the Internet, people can access almost all of human knowledge instantaneously and from anywhere.

For Gen Y, it's natural to be able to pull back and see multiple perspectives from a variety of cultures and belief systems. And they're able to respond to any kind of change and embrace it because they see how the changes going on globally are all interrelated. Humans literally didn't have this capacity before.

Gen Y Project:

Yes. I understand what you are saying. When I ask Baby Boomers and some Gen Xers what they think will happen in the future, they will try to predict. When I ask Gen Y leaders the same question, every single one tells me that they won't even try to guess; they'll just say that the world is going to change and it's going to change very quickly, so just be prepared for things to be different when you wake up tomorrow morning.

Kent, when you look at designing an experience for people, what are some of the things you consider?

Kent:

I intend to change the questions that people are asking themselves. I purposely work to take on as many perspectives as I can — the person who's going to watch it, the operator that's going to run it, the developer that is going to build it, and so on. I want everyone involved with the experience to find themselves asking questions they had never thought about asking prior to experiencing whatever I created for them. More than anything, I want to create experiences where people have the opportunity to create as much depth in their own interaction with it as possible. I design experiences to give people choice.

Gen Y Project:

I know you've worked on the fountains at Bellagio. What thinking went into that experience?

Kent:

The Bellagio Fountains is still one of my favorite projects; they literally stop traffic. In other words, people drive by and stop in the middle of the road to see it. People have a choice about how they interact with it.

The original intention was to create beauty and entertainment, as well as an icon that would draw people into the hotel, whether they saw it live or on TV or in a movie. And it does that very effectively. The somewhat unintended effect is that the fountains don't just entertain people, but they can cause you to pause and connect with yourself and something beautiful in one of the most distracting environments on the planet.

Every time I'm in Las Vegas, I go to see the fountains. I like to know what new songs they've added, and how the shows have changed. Mostly, I go to watch the people who are watching the show.

Once I met a couple there in their early 20s from Britain. They come to Vegas every year, not to gamble but to see what's new in Las Vegas —

new hotels, new restaurants, and new shows. And the Bellagio Fountains are their favorite thing. They come out every night watch the fountains! And I learned something very valuable from them. They didn't watch them to be entertained so much as they wanted to study them.

Our intent with the Fountains wasn't to create something that people could sit and study and be fascinated by how it works, but that's exactly what this couple did. That's now an element that I have as a goal with my all designs today — providing people an opportunity to pull the curtain back and to discover how something works. Sometimes people want the illusion. Sometimes they want to know how it works. I design to give them the choice.

Gen Y Project:

Knowing how your customers relate to your creations, how do you design an experience that excites them?

Kent:

There's a practice called "interaction design" that I employ. I create spaces and experiences that limit your choices. Now, I said earlier that I design to give people choice. So there's a paradox of both creating choice and limiting choices. I design to provide limited meaningful choices rather than numerous meaningless choices.

A business wants to encourage a particular outcome for the audience, whether it's a purchase or a particular decision. And interaction design, purposely creating limited meaningful choices, is a way of achieving this business goal.

When you walk into stores that are popular with Gen Y, it's like being in a club with music that's really pumping and loud. So they make a distinction in designing their stores. They're trying to attract people that are comfortable with a high energy, loud environment and then once a cus-

tomer is in the store, there's a lot of space for people to make their own choices with how they interact there. Their target customers self-select themselves by choosing to enter the environment or not.

Gen Y Project:

We think our subtle actions aren't being noticed, but it's the little things that people do notice — more often than we realize. There are people who actually study your subtle approaches to see if you're someone they want to do business with. Are you finding this is also true for Gen Y?

Kent:

Absolutely, and this goes back to that emotional authenticity we were talking about before. Gen Y wants to be able to make choices, yet they're comfortable with not knowing crystal clear answers before they make a decision. There's been a shift from where people want to have a clear answer, black and white, what they did and didn't like. With Gen Y, they're really comfortable with ambiguity, with not knowing exactly what an outcome is going to look like or be like. Again, it's being able to take perspectives and choose and shift along the spectrum of experience and culture to see where they fit at a particular moment.

Gen Y Project:

I hear the comment that Generation Y is entitled and very often, they even come across to older leaders as being lazy. What are your thoughts on that view?

Kent:

I disagree. Gen Y knows they don't have to work hard. Gen Y has never really known adversity or poverty close at hand; it's on TV, but it is something they've never had to experience. And there's a huge amount of evidence that big shifts around the world mean that Gen Y doesn't have to worry about some of the issues the previous generations did. For example, armed conflict has declined 40 percent in the last 20 years; poverty has decreased, and we don't hear a lot about that on the news.

So, Gen Y has the freedom to know that they can work smarter and not harder; they want to work mentally and not physically. It isn't, "Do I want to work 40 or 50 or 60 hours a week at a corporate job?" but "What's the purpose of my life and where can I invest my time and make a difference in the world?" They also think about things like: Are they going to be a voyeur? Do they want to jump in and comment, or do they want to influence and invent the experiences and spaces they're involved in?

Gen Y Project:

How do you see this new era of choice playing out?

Kent:

Gen Y has a choice about their influence. They can choose whether they want to directly influence the outcome of something that's happening around them or if they want to see where it goes. Take American Idol, for example; that's not just a TV show people watch. If they want to influence the selection, they can actually vote. And in almost any kind of interaction online, they can choose who they show up as. Do they want to show up as themselves or as an avatar? Do they want to be identified anonymously or be part of a group? They can choose the experience.

Gen Y Project:

I'm interested in the way you design transformational experiences for people. How do you go about transforming people's thinking and behaviors?

Kent:

That is the billion-dollar question, right? We're in this "experience econ-omy" and transformation is at the top of the experience hierarchy. People have always loved to learn, and now Gen Y is in a position to exercise that choice. Learning to them is more important than gaining status sym-bols or money, so you see this huge movement of all these transforma-tional products and services that are catering to that.

There's a fascinating book called Everything Bad is Good for You *by Steven Johnson, where he took the assumption that pop culture over the past 30 years has degraded society's morals and those things like video games and MTV are making people more stupid rather than smarter. He found that IQs have increased 15 to 20 points on average in the U.S. — that things like video games are actually training people how to think in far more complex ways than before.*

The more you can engage people's desire to learn, and the deeper the level of complexity, whether conscious or unconscious, the more powerful the experience. When you give people the opportunity to dive down the rab-bit hole and go as deep as they want to go, you create the opportunity for a deep meaningful connection to something that's important to them.

Gen Y Project:

Don't ever underestimate the power of an experience. In Dr. Jean Twenge's book, Generation Me, *she calls Gen Y one of the loneliest, depressed gen-erations in history. They are craving public and social interaction.*

I think what we are learning is that there is a resurgence of people con-necting to online communities for social interaction and then forming local communities or attending live events. People do crave human, face to face interactions

Let's talk about this experience economy. Where is Gen Y taking us next?

Kent:

It's a relatively new phenomenon that's being studied academically and applied in business. There's a European Center for the Experience Economy based in Amsterdam that is a mix of business and academic research on where experiences are going. I see it all pouring into deeper and deeper levels of meaning and authenticity. Ultimately, this study and application can predictably drive people to retail centers or entertainment attractions and can help cause their meaningful experiences with others.

An offshoot of that is an emerging economy of attention, where you create experiences to capture and keep people's attention and interest. Beyond that, I see an expansion to an economy of influence — not on a big governmental institution kind of level, but influence in a social network, which exists both online and offline. From a shopping standpoint, Gen Y is far more apt to act on the recommendations of people they haven't met but are in a social network with than they are any kind of advertising or in-store promotion.

So, being able to trade and traffic and influence is where I think Gen Y is going to continue to expand, not only in terms of shopping, but what the world is focusing its attention on. You can look at the ONE campaign for a current example of this.

Gen Y Project:

Kent, what is your vision for Live Experience Design in the future?

Kent:

I look for intersections to work in. Money and creativity is a great intersection; it's why I lived in Las Vegas for so many years. Now I'm building a business at the intersection of global communications technology, conscious capitalism, and meaningful entertaining experiences. Live Experience Design will be a global leader in creating meaningful relevant experiences that cause people to choose to make a difference in the world.

POINTS FOR REFLECTION

 That value of an experience has elevated to the point that consumers already expect businesses to orchestrate events that invite interaction in a way that touches them emotionally and on a deeply meaningful level. Engaging the five senses isn't enough. What can you do to engage people emotionally, intellectually, and socially?

 Gen Y is so deluged with information and sensory noise that you need to continually challenge your questions in order to deliver memorable results. You can create sensations for people, or you can create spaces for them to explore what they're sensing. The more you can interact with your customers or audience members (playing games, telling stories, engaging in artistic activities), the greater your chance to make a lasting impression on them. How can you enhance the experience to make a more powerful impression?

 Each time you design a new experience, product, or service for your customers or audience, ask yourself this question: How can I change the questions people are asking me? Inspire curiosity? Create intrigue? Consider the questions you want people to ask. Then create an experience that will allow those questions to bubble up to the surface.

 Each time we try something new or enter the unknown, we reward ourselves with new sensations that strengthen the physical, mental, emotional, and spiritual components of life. By learning how to be comfortable with ambiguity, you will find that you also open yourself up to new experiences. What new territories can you explore?

Walt Disney said, "Animation offers a medium of storytelling and visual entertainment that can bring pleasure and information to people of all ages everywhere in the world." By focusing on creating excitement, what are some specific ways you can contribute to a richer and more meaningful life for those people whose lives you touch?

ABOUT KENT CORBELL

A self-confessed "A/V kid," **Kent Corbell** now plays in the space where design, entertainment, communications, business, and architecture meet. He has toured with Lynyrd Skynyrd and George Clinton, been a stagehand at Walt Disney World, engineered sound systems in Korea, designed theme parks in Taiwan, and has contributed to several major projects in Las Vegas. Kent leads Live Experience Design, a global experience creation company. He is currently writing a book on the elements of creating and marketing with extraordinary experiences. For more information, visit www.liveexperiencedesign.com.

» PART FOUR «

Gen Y In The Workplace

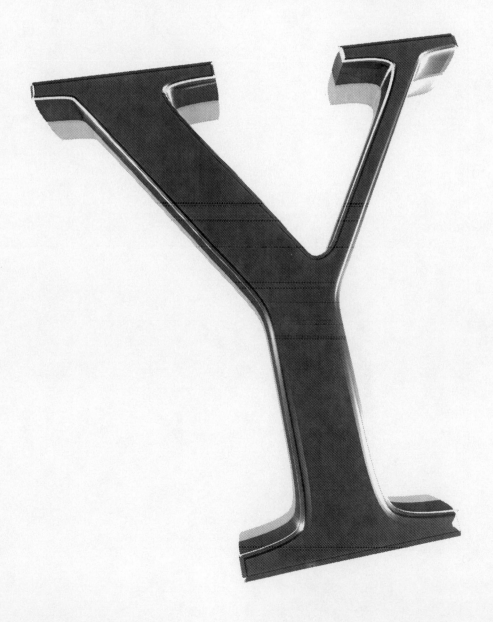

» CHAPTER 18 «

The Generational Workforce: Peter Sheahan

"Having fun and work is not an oxymoron for Gen Y."

Gen Y has brought a new attitude to the workplace and created a major stir in the way employers hire and manage their workers. Conventional practices for hiring and retaining good employees doesn't work for this generation of job-hoppers whose criteria for selecting a job is so unique that employers are adopting a concierge mentality to appeal to them. So, it's time to take a fresh look at not only how we market to this generation as a consumer, but also as a prospective employee.

Peter Sheahan is a recognized leader in generational change and workforce trends. The Australian native is the author of numerous books on Gen Y, including *Generation Y: Thriving and Surviving with Gen Y at Work*. He has extensively studied the traits and attitudes of Gen Y as they affect the workplace and this generation's impact on consumerism. Peter works all over the world, with clients such as Google, BMW, L'Oreal, and Ernst & Young.

With guidance from Peter, employers can begin to understand this emerging workforce, and Gen Y can grasp the challenges they present to their employers.

Gen Y Project:

Peter, in your books about Gen Y, you present the perspective that we shouldn't think of Gen Y as a group but as an emerging mindset. Can you explain this position?

Peter:

If you think about generational modeling, it's like reading your horoscope in the newspaper and believing what you read. So, to suggest that the 70 million plus people born in the U.S. from 1978 to 1994 are exactly the same is obviously a flawed concept. What you're talking about with generational modeling is shifting the bell curve. That bell curve is in a slightly different place in terms of bandwidth than it may have been for Generation X or the Baby Boomers.

Not everyone perfectly fits the model, but we're looking for evidence of social change — shifts in expectations in the way employees show up for work, in the way they need to be sold to, etc. What we're noticing — not just in the U.S., but also Australia, China and parts of Europe as well — is that the expectations of Gen Y are trending upwards. The products, brands, and services that the late teens/early 20s markets are embracing are also being embraced by the late 20s, 30s and even early 40s markets.

Gen Y Project:

How does this shift affect the workplace?

Peter:

If you look at the last few years, there's been a lot of talk about how demanding Gen Y is with their employers about (1) creating an environment that's nurturing, transparent, collaborative, collegial, etc.; and (2) workplaces that care about social causes and the environment. You now look at the behavior of Gen X and the Baby Boomers, and it's starting to reflect their expectations, too. Add to that the tightening labor market, particularly in Western developed countries, and you find the good candidates are in the box seats — they negotiate the terms of whom they work for and how. Also, it's not just Gen Y that is becoming harder and harder to attract, engage and retain, but other generations are also proving more difficult to attract.

Gen Y Project:

I've read one of your white papers about the way we sell to this audience. You had an interesting observation that Gen Y is either thinking car or career.

Peter:

That's actually a metaphor that Eric Chester coined. When you employ a younger person in the U.S., they're either doing it for the money, or they're genuinely doing it for the career. In the U.S., particularly those that are college educated, they're thinking more about their career, whereas in other parts of the world, Gen Y's are just jumping from job to job. In fact, we're even seeing where they're leaving serious positions to work in entry-level jobs — the local gas station, for example, because all they want is enough money to surf or buy a car.

Gen Y Project:

How will this value-shift change the way businesses market to them?

Peter:

Let me tell you a bit of story to introduce how we're changing the way we market. It relates to the way employers are marketing themselves because the big workforce trend over the next 5-10 years will be employment branding: how an organization positions itself as an outstanding place to work. Organizations like Google tell a great story and then let

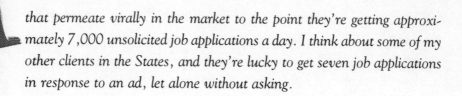

that permeate virally in the market to the point they're getting approximately 7,000 unsolicited job applications a day. I think about some of my other clients in the States, and they're lucky to get seven job applications in response to an ad, let alone without asking.

Gen Y Project:

So, employers need to brand their workplace to prospective employees and treat them like a consumer? That's a fascinating shift! How should an employer look at this new model?

Peter:

The customer today demands four things, and I want to first talk about three of those four: fast, good, and cheap. That is, they want good products at a great price — meaning value for money — and they want them now. This is especially true of Gen Y, who has a compressed view of time. The idea of instant gratification is very prevalent in a consumer as well as an employee. If you relate fast, good, and cheap to the employment landscape, you start realizing that "good" means they want to work in a company with a good reputation. When you correlate "cheap" to the employment context, we want to be well rewarded for a job well done — we want fair compensation, basically. Then if you look at "fast," it means very distinct things: the speed with which it engages — which is the recruitment process — and the speed with which they progress Gen Y through the organization.

Gen Y Project:

This impatience is definitely a dominant trait with Gen Y.

Peter:

The biggest challenge I've seen in North American work forces is Gen Y's impatience about how quickly they progress through the work place.

They have organizations telling them "One day, this could all be yours," but that "one day" is in 24 years. Your 25-year-old, bright young person isn't going to wait that long to get that opportunity. Once upon a time, good compensation might have made up for a company that wasn't as great to work for or, in a great organization, it made up for the fact that you had some slow internal processes — you didn't get promoted as quickly — but the company looked good on your resume.

Now we're seeing Gen Y demand all three, and that's not what even distinguishes one workplace from another or one product from another. Today, the consumer is looking for the "fourth dimension" of competitive advantage — and when I say "consumer," I'm talking about the employee as well as the buyer.

Gen Y Project:

If fast, good, and cheap are the first three, what is the fourth dimension?

Peter:

It's tied up in to what Joe Pine discussed in The Experience Economy, which talks about how you create a consumer experience. That is, employers and retailers are trying to offer a sensory experience to their employees and customers, and they haven't done a good job with that, in my opinion. Consumers want good products that are priced well that they get quickly, but they also want ones that don't damage the environment. Look at the Wal-Mart push towards green and how they design their stores; it's about building an environment that's a great place to shop and work.

Gen Y is looking for experiences that inspire them. If you look at Apple's design-based strategy, it's about how they inspire people. As Steve Jobs said, "The way you can tell if it's good is if you want to lick the screen." You only have to think about how obsessive Apple users are to affirm the success of Apple's strategy. And it's not just Apple, but also Samsung, who's designing products that people want to look at and touch. Consider

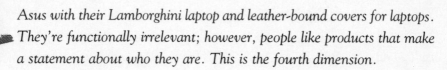

Asus with their Lamborghini laptop and leather-bound covers for laptops. They're functionally irrelevant; however, people like products that make a statement about who they are. This is the fourth dimension.

It's about products that integrate into their lives. There's a lot of talk how iPod's design and headphones made it a success. In my opinion, what made them a success was iTunes. It was the Gen Xers desperately holding on to their youth that bought the first iPod. The functionality of iTunes really drove its success.

Gen Y Project:

When I look at some of the new technology coming out today, the whole design element is changing because of what Apple has done. Would you agree? Even the iTunes commercials make dancing alone look really cool.

Peter:

I agree with that, but if you look at what took the iPod mainstream — because it is a mainstream product — it's not just design. When you talk about the campaign of dancing by yourself, it's part of the social identity theory, and we're seeing more of that with Gen Y.

Gen Y Project:

Tell us more about social identity theory and about the social identity of Gen Y.

Peter:

Social identity theory is we take jobs, buy clothes, and support brands and labels because of the statement it says to the world; marketers call this "aspirational consumption" — we buy something because we want to make a statement about who we are.

We're seeing a shift with Gen Y where it's not about buying products or brands based on what it says to the world; it's as much about the statement it says to you about you. I was at a jewelry design boutique in San Francisco looking at a rubber bracelet that was interesting. I was told it was $5,000 and I thought, "It's just a piece of rubber." The guy at the counter said, "It's not a piece of rubber; it's a 24 karat solid gold band covered in rubber." He told me, "The people who buy these products aren't doing it to make a statement to the world; they're buying it to make a statement to themselves."

Gen Y Project:

So it's more about showing off to yourself than trying to impress the rest of the world?

Peter:

Traditional social identity theory was about the aspirational outside, where Gen Y is starting to look at aspirational inside. Look at the growth of yoga, fitness programs, and organic food. People are embracing these things because they want to become more of who they are rather than a fake identity they're trying to portray to the world.

To go back to your first question about Gen Y as an emerging mindset, it's not just about the Gen Yers — it's also the Gen Xers and the Boomers embracing that.

I've been involved in a big piece of research called "NEO consumers" which was founded by two Aussies. In conjunction with Roy Morgan Research, they developed a very powerful customer typology that's much more indicative of people's spending behaviors than the income they earn. We've been examining Gen Y NEO's — there are about 20 million in the U.S. These are the aspirational inside consumers; we're seeing these trendsetters on the fringe of society buying these rubber bracelets because they're gold on the inside.

Gen Y Project:

It speaks to the whole transparency and authenticity in marketing. Would you agree?

Peter:

Yes. Authenticity is a big part of marketing brands to Gen Y. Just look at the success of Jake Burton. He was one of the first entrepreneurs to sell these snowboard contraptions 30 years ago around Vermont; he doesn't sponsor the events — he started them. We certainly see Gen Y embracing those kinds of brands.

Gen Y Project:

We've been talking about the authenticity and integrity of this group. Where is this shift headed after authenticity?

Peter:

That is a good question. If we could get to genuine transparency and authenticity in 10 or 20 years, I'd be over the moon. Authenticity is about being open to the feedback from the market and being honest in the communication. You only have to look at some of the marketing from the Detroit automakers to see that it was GM that went after the crowdsourcing model when they created an ad for their SUV. Crowdsourcing gave consumers and low paid volunteers the opportunity to have a voice in product development and design. The consumers really tore strips off those guys.

Gen Y Project:

And they took that whole campaign down, right?

Peter:

Well, they took down the bits that were offensive, but I wouldn't be sur-prised if by now they've completely ripped it off the table. That told them they were way off trend, and the customer is saying this isn't what they want. For a big company with all kinds of money tied up in their market-ing, this message wasn't something they wanted to hear.

Gen Y Project:

Are there other priorities in the Gen Y consumer mindset that businesses need to recognize in order to strengthen their marketing to this segment?

Peter:

Easy is the next big priority. Fifteen years ago, cost was the primary source of competitive advantage. In many ways, our growing affluence has meant that "share of wallet" is less a priority for many consumers, unless, of course, the product is not differentiated. So if we are not con-cerned with money alone, what are we concerned with? I think people are looking for an easier life.

In my mind, one of the key ways we market products and job opportu-nities is how easily our opportunities integrate into the lives of the people we're trying to recruit or sell to. That is, how neutral is our product, our service, our brand on the mental energy of the person? I don't mean men-tal capacity — how we get their attention — it's more like the iTunes thing. It works, it's easy, it's plug and play, and I think that's going to be a big frontier in the next few years. I know, for example, geographic loca-tion is proving to be a big hindrance for many companies operating in more isolated areas — more so today than 10 years ago.

Gen Y Project:

Can you see any other trends that smart entrepreneurs should watch?

Peter:

I think the big trend will be not just experiences from a fun point of view, but experiences that change the way people view the world. Life coaching is an example; I also made the point about yoga being so popular. It helps you feel better, act better, and live better. I think that idea of transformation is starting to get real traction now. For example, what Cirque du Soleil has done is not just create a great entertainment experience; they've created a life changing experience. There's something about pushing human potential — they do things you thought people would never do.

There are three other things that seem to be getting traction from a consumer point of view. One is beauty. I know a law firm in LA that pays their graduates $160,000 a year straight out of college but felt the need to redesign their offices so they would be nicer to look at. This pay scale is huge for an entry level position, but the law firm felt that they still needed to redesign their offices to make them more beautiful...the high salary ranges are not enough to attract Gen Y.

Another is responsibility — how you behave in the marketplace and the communities that you serve. An example of that is a bank here in Australia that signed what is called "the equator principles," agreeing not to fund any project that would have a negative impact on the environment in the community in which they operated. This is proving very successful in their marketing to staff and customers.

The last one is fun. An escape from the grind of day-to-day life is going to be increasingly more valuable. I think Gen Y is going to have quarter-life crises where if their life hasn't panned out how they thought by age 25, they're going to engage in more and more extreme activities just for an escape.

Gen Y Project:

If you can make the work experience more fun, challenging, and inspiring, you're more likely to attract quality people. It sounds like Gen Y is asking that everyday life be the same.

Peter:

Having fun and work is not an oxymoron for Gen Y. Say you come out of Yale and you're in the top of your law class and you have six or seven offers — all from great firms with great starting salaries. How are you going to distinguish whether you pick law firm A or law firm B? It's going to sit in these superficial areas, because most other things like reputation and remuneration will be equal. You're going for the one you'll fit into best, the most fun place to work.

Gen Y Project:

What happens after they get into that experience? Is it fun or "now you've got to go to work"?

Peter:

Herein lies the problem. With a shortage of quality candidates, you'll do anything to get them. The more you inflate the actual experience, the more you lead to incorrect expectations and that leads to rapid disengagement. It's a huge concern.

Gen Y Project:

I know that the whole Web 2.0 thing is a big issue, but I'm seeing more Baby Boomers and even Gen Xers saying they're not going to get involved in that.

Peter:

There are a couple reasons why people are a little afraid of Web 2.0. Essentially, it's user-generated content. YouTube, MySpace, or Facebook don't create content; they facilitate the user's ability to create content and that's what has been coined as Web 2.0. If you go to the MIT media labs, they're talking Web 3.0 and 4.0.

People should be wary about getting into these environments, and one reason is ultimate transparency. It's a very open and honest or sometimes "in your face" kind of environment. It's not just about fear of technology, but it's a genuine protection of their brand.

Gen Y Project:

Don't you think it works both ways? If you had a great experience, or if you are authentic and have a great product, this viral communication is going to accelerate delivery of that message, too.

Peter:

If you have a good experience in a restaurant, you tell two or three people; if you have a bad experience, they say you tell 10 or 11. Well, if you're Gen Y and you're online, you tell 10,000. You only have to tell it once and the virus spreads. Web 2.0 is an intensified version of word-of-mouth — the higher tech version of the local market where you hear all the gossip — but it's gossip on steroids.

POINTS FOR REFLECTION

As you are considering a career path, seek out an environment where creativity and independent thinking are both encouraged and championed.

 During the interview process, examine the culture. Is it transparent, nurturing, collegial, and inspiring? If not, keep looking for a work culture that will provide the type of environment that gives you the opportunity to be both challenged and supported.

 Ask your potential employer about the work flow and process. Does the company offer flex hours, the ability to telecommute, and the opportunity to travel?

 As a Generation Y young adult, you place a high value on self-fulfillment. When considering career, travel, and personal choices, be sure to take into consideration those options that allow you to become more of who you are.

 If you are marketing to Gen Y, look closely at your products and services and how you are recruiting Gen Y workers. Answer these four questions: Is it fast? Is it good? Is it cheap? Does it offer a great experience? If so — and you've been honest in your responses – you are on the right path in marketing to Gen Y.

ABOUT PETER SHEAHAN

Peter Sheahan is a global consultant and a leader in generational workforces and change. A former Young Entrepreneur of the Year (2003), he was also chosen by his peers at the National Speakers Association of Australia as the 2006 Keynote Speaker of the Year. Peter is the author of *The Generation Y: Thriving and Surviving with Generation Y at Work*, and his newest release, *Flip*. His books and more information about his consulting services are available at www.petersheahan.com.

» CHAPTER 19 «

Inspirion, Inc.: Misti Burmeister

"We all want to feel like we matter. That doesn't change, no matter what generation you're in."

Generation Y has its signature traits, but how does this collection of habits, interests, tendencies, and desires translate into working well with others? How can you effectively blend the differences in motivation and work ethic? Can their sociological culture blend with the corporate culture, where four generations co-exist? What gets them motivated? What frustrates or bores them, and where they can benefit from the more experienced colleague?

Misti Burmeister is an energetic, motivated coach who has focused her career on the problem of and solution for blending multi-generations in the workplace. She has developed a solid approach to building workplace relations. As CEO of Inspirion Inc., Misti's inter-generational coaching within corporations has proven to be effective in reducing turnover among younger workers. She facilitates communication between younger staff and more seasoned management that results in more productive and effective work environments.

Misti's collaborative approach provides a practical blueprint for developing young leaders and building strong teams. She has spent over a decade studying and working with these new employees, helping them to reach their potential and overcome the challenges

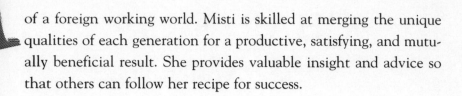

of a foreign working world. Misti is skilled at merging the unique qualities of each generation for a productive, satisfying, and mutually beneficial result. She provides valuable insight and advice so that others can follow her recipe for success.

Gen Y Project:

You came upon the leadership role by circumstance, more than intention. Tell us where this began for you.

Misti:

I came to Washington, D.C., to take a fellowship with the National Institutes of Health. Before that, I spent six years at the University of Northern Colorado leading and mentoring my fellow students. I taught classes in this while I was getting my undergraduate degrees in kinesiology and psychology.

Gen Y Project:

Your career began while you were still in college. This is a trend we're seeing in Gen Y. I understand that once you left this environment, you began seeking out mentors to help you make some key decisions for your life. Was this helpful?

Misti:

In one year, I went through five mentors, not because I wanted to, but because they did not know what to do with all my energy, excitement, and enthusiasm, which many young people today certainly have. I would go sit in front of these mentors and say, "Okay, where am I going? What do I need to do? Who do I need to meet?" Inevitably, they would say "Here's about 60 hours of work to do behind the desk; please get out of my office." So, I would go on to the next mentor.

Gen Y Project:

So, it wasn't necessarily mentoring that fell short of your desires, but the lack of the right matches. But after your fellowship, when you moved to D.C., did you discover a different environment there?

Misti:

The story was pretty much the same. In the company where I was working, I didn't have a team of people to work with and I was in a city where I knew virtually no one. So, I researched the whole company and read nearly every document they'd put out through the media. I did this in about 3 1/2? weeks and presented a plan to the head of the company about how to best leverage my skill set. At the end of my presentation, she said, "It's clear you have problems with anxiety. Do you take medication for that?"

Gen Y Project:

How did you respond to that?

Misti:

I don't believe she meant it in a negative way; she just didn't know what to do with my energy and enthusiasm. The next day, I turned in my letter of resignation. I firmly believed that there was a disconnect between myself and my two previous employers because I believed in my heart that they really wanted to help me and I knew I wanted to help them and be helped by them. It was crystal clear that my passion was most connected to helping young professionals to develop their leadership and even more important than that, helping people from different generations communicate with each other.

Gen Y Project:

So you are really honed in on both teaching older generations how to train and work with younger generations and then working with the Gen Y's

to develop their skills to be successful. Since they come from different mindsets, it must be a challenge to bridge this gap.

Misti:

I firmly believe that the only way the younger generation is going to be able to gain the wisdom and knowledge of the older generation is to be able to speak the same language — to understand each other.

Gen Y Project:

Can you offer a brief snapshot of the four generations and some of the common values?

Misti:

Let me start with the "Silent Generation." The birthdates for that are 1922 to 1943, which means they're 64 to 84. If you just think globally what was happening in the world when they were coming into the workforce, there was the great depression, World War II, and the Korean War, so naturally most of the men were off fighting and most of the women stayed behind taking care of the homes and the homeland while they were gone, which is, by the way, what got the women their start in the workplace.

As a result, some of their core values are civic pride, loyalty, respect for authority, dedication, and sacrifice, and so forth. They're the kind of people that really want to go in and do a great job and just keep quiet. They're very grateful to have a job in the first place. They're driven by duty before pleasure, which is the opposite of the youngest generation.

Gen Y Project:

This generation is now exiting the workplace. What influence do they still have on others today?

Misti:

This generation is great in terms of mentorship. They're no longer in the mix of things on a daily basis; they're in more of a consulting role, which lends itself naturally to do more mentoring without this pressure about someone taking their job.

Gen Y Project:

So the Silent Generation won the wars. What shaped the next generation, the Baby Boomers who were born between 1943 and 1960?

Misti:

Most of the wars — the big wars — were pretty much complete and there was extreme optimism and hope. The Baby Boomers were shaped by the landing on the moon, the Peace Corps — certainly the Vietnam War is not to be excluded — as well as Woodstock and the civil rights movement. Working hard to get ahead is very much a part of this generation's language. They want to provide more to their children than what their parents did, and they want to do better than their parents did.

Gen Y Project:

As a result of this desire to be better providers, the Baby Boomers developed the dual-income household. This certainly impacted the workplace dynamic. In fact, although we credit Gen Y with being extreme entrepreneurs, they actually had a strong role model.

Misti:

The research shows that Baby Boomer women are the ones who are starting their own companies more than any other group.

Gen Y Project:

The sheer size of this Baby Boomer generation, 74 million, also had a tremendous impact on the workforce. They became trendsetters by virtue of the vast size of their population

Misti:

Yes. I will also add that many organizations look to them and what their interests are to create products that will meet their wants and needs, because they do make up a huge portion of our buying population.

Gen Y Project:

Now Baby Boomers are beginning to retire as well. What affect will this have on the Gen X and Gen Y workers remaining?

Misti:

Research has shown that for every two Baby Boomers that leave the workforce, only one Generation Yer comes in to fill the slot. That's a pretty big difference in terms of size of generation. Generation Xers are mostly in the mid-management positions, sandwiched between two different generations that are both bigger than they are.

Gen Y Project:

So, let's look at these Gen Xers. They were born between 1960 and 1980, which means they're 27 to 47. What has shaped their culture?

Misti:

Some of the events were Watergate, the Challenger disaster, terrorism, and computers. They were left to fend for themselves and surf the Web. As a result, they've developed the need for constant stimulation, instant gratification, and independence. This isn't right or wrong; it's just what's there.

Gen Y Project:

What is their workplace mindset?

Misti:

They want to be asked questions, rather than just being fed information. They really believe that their opinions should matter. Most Generation Xers don't have the sense that authority is something to be afraid of; they have no sense of sensitivity to rank at all. They have a huge distaste of micromanagement. They want you to give them what they need to do, a target date, and then they want to go out and do it.

Gen Y Project:

This brings us to Gen Y, which is comprised of people born between 1980 and 2000. Tell us about their upbringing and how it has created their work ethic.

Misti:

This generation was raised in the high tech world for sure; they grew up with hyper-involved parents and overscheduled lives. They're used to being seen and heard all the time. This generation is known for just walking into the CEO's office and saying, "I don't want to do this," and they're also known for hopping from job to job.

Gen Y Project:

Is that because they were trained to behave this way by parents and other authority figures? Or are other things contributing to these characteristics?

Misti:

Possibly. I would say they're mostly doing it because they don't know what they want to go after or there's something they don't like about

223 «

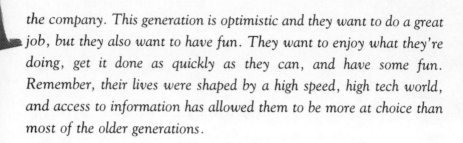

the company. This generation is optimistic and they want to do a great job, but they also want to have fun. They want to enjoy what they're doing, get it done as quickly as they can, and have some fun. Remember, their lives were shaped by a high speed, high tech world, and access to information has allowed them to be more at choice than most of the older generations.

Gen Y Project:

What are some of the problems organizations are facing when communicating with these twenty-something leaders?

Misti:

Many organizations, especially those that are sales-related, are trying to speak to these people with the wrong mindset. One of the executives I coach recently said to me, "These young people text message and Email like crazy" and this is in sales, but they won't go out and have a face to face with the client. The way Gen Y communicates is so different than older generations. It is certainly something to recognize as an opportunity for training and development for Gen Y.

Gen Y Project:

So you need to effectively coach both sides here, but how do you bring them together?

Misti:

I help them with people skills and I'll coach that executive on how they can teach young professionals, which has everything to do with teaching them the skills that they're missing. The greatest challenge I see with seasoned professionals is their unwillingness to take the time to coach or mentor young professionals. They want young professionals to simply "get it" without taking the time to show them. What they don't understand is that taking the time to coach or mentor them will, in the end, save them a great deal of time.

Gen Y Project:

Can you give an example of the skills they lack?

Misti:

I was at a CEO's office in DC about two years ago and she said to me, "I can't believe I just hired this young person and for their first meeting, they came into my office without a piece of paper or a pen in their hand." I asked, "What did you make that to mean?" She had a laundry list of things she made it mean and I then said, "What if it just means she didn't know?"

Gen Y Project:

So it's purely a lack of awareness on the part of the Gen Y.

Misti:

Don't take it personally; they're not meaning to annoy you at all. If they're not dressed in appropriate clothing, find a way to share that with them. If they're not showing up for work on time, I would say to give them the critical feedback they need. If they need training on how to effectively network face to face, take them with you to a networking event. Help them to build that support network. Help them to find mentors. Help them to fall flat on their face, and then help them through it. Finally, have fun with them.

Gen Y Project:

What other challenges do Gen Yers face in being successful as a professional?

Misti:

I would say patience. They grew up in a world of instant gratification; they saw the beginning and the end, but they didn't see what it takes to get there. Inside their minds, they believe that they should be somewhere they're not. They also lack understanding of who they are. If you don't know who you are and you're not self-assured, it's difficult to be a leader for someone else.

Gen Y Project:

You mentioned that the Silent Generation leaders are excellent at mentoring. How can this help Gen Y?

Misti:

Gen Y's lack mentorship. They don't know how to ask more seasoned people for help; it somehow means something bad about them. I say to them, "Don't be afraid to ask for help. Ask them how you can get better."

Gen Y Project:

Baby Boomers are big on leaving a legacy, everything from leaving money for their kids to building a wing at the church or planting trees on their block and having them named after their family. Could mentoring be a type of legacy?

Misti:

Yes. Inside the workforce, get the Baby Boomers to mentor other people — that's leaving a legacy.

Gen Y Project:

Job-hopping is another trait that appears consistently among this generation. What does this convey about Gen Y to the older generations that share their workplace?

Misti:

When you jump from job to job it speaks volumes to your commitment and demonstrates your impatience. Spending six months to a year in an organization is not really enough time to understand how things flow. Again, sticking with a job long enough to truly learn from it can teach a young leader both about patience and the benefits of perseverance.

Gen Y Project:

I've heard that you can't get too hip or too savvy with Gen Y because they'll see right through it.

Misti:

They can smell inauthenticity from a mile away. Be honest with them. I'd also say assume they have something to offer to the conversation. You might get something from them, but more important, they hear you saying, "What you have to say matters." We all want to feel like we're engaged in the world; we all want to feel like we matter. It's no different, whatever generation you're in.

Gen Y Project:

Is there one message that is critical for the generations in the workplace?

Misti:

Listen to your passion. Stop and take a minute and look within and make sure you're going after what you truly love to do. If you don't know why you're doing what you're doing, it's very easy to be shaken up and tossed aside. Conversely, when you're clear about your career direction, you can stay focused on that and let the rest take care of itself. If you're not yet clear, take time to reflect, begin asking questions and gain clarity regarding your strengths. While your long-term vision may not come over night, it will come over time ~ start the process today.

POINTS FOR REFLECTION

 Choosing the right career path will establish the foundation for happiness in your life. Before you make that commitment, look closely at organizations and career opportunities that line up with your passion and will allow you to leverage your talents and assets.

 Success in the corporate world requires you to communicate with people outside your comfort zone: other generations with different perspectives, thoughts processes, and life experiences. By making the effort to better understand each generation and the world events that shaped their lives, you can develop a more effective, productive, and harmonious work environment.

 Recognize key differences in communication style. Don't assume that text messaging or email is the preferred method; when in doubt, just ask. Be flexible, respectful, and tolerant of these differences.

 Don't be afraid to ask questions. Self-reliance is a wonderful skill, but it can also hold you back from getting answers that can forward your life and career.

 When considering leaving a job for greener pastures, stop and ask yourself these questions: "What am I truly looking to achieve by moving on to this next job?" and "What can I learn by staying where I am?" Perseverance is a skill shared by some of the greatest leaders of our time, and loyalty to a company can yield great benefits down the road (including strengthening relationships, strong recommendations and the ability to expand your network).

ABOUT MISTI BURMEISTER

Misti Burmeister earned a Master's degree in human communication, with an emphasis in leadership and health communication, a blend of mind and body. With over a decade of experience, she's an expert on coaching and empowering Generations X and Y in their professional careers through individual and corporate coaching, speaking, and emerging leader seminars. Misti has been awarded the eWomen Network's prestigious International Award for Emerging Leaders. She was also named a Fellow at the Foundation for Community Leadership as an acknowledgment for her commitment and vision to inter-generational teams and leaders. For more information, visit her website: www.inspirioninc.com.

Y

» CHAPTER 20 «

"My Reality Check Bounced":
Jason Dorsey

*"The tough wake-up call is when you eventually
realize that the paths that make you financially rich
or give you a big title may not ultimately make you
happy. That's just hard for us to accept."*

We already know that Gen Yers live by a different set of rules than other generations. They have higher expectations that set them apart and present a significant set of challenges, both for themselves as employees seeking instant gratification and for the employers who want to get the most from them, including retaining the good ones!

Jason Dorsey is an energetic Gen Y leader and author who has been lauded by such renowned professionals as Stephen Covey, Jack Canfield, and Po Bronson. He began to shape his future at 14 by exploring different career opportunities. By 18, Jason had already done incredible work on what it means to take control of your life. In 2004, he won the Austin Under 40 Entrepreneur of the Year Award in the Education category, when he was 25. Previous recipients include Michael Dell and Lance Armstrong. And, at 28, Dorsey had already authored four books and been featured on 20/20, NBC's Today Show, and ABC's The View.

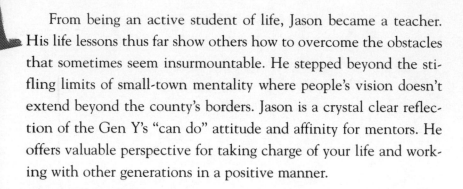

From being an active student of life, Jason became a teacher. His life lessons thus far show others how to overcome the obstacles that sometimes seem insurmountable. He stepped beyond the stifling limits of small-town mentality where people's vision doesn't extend beyond the county's borders. Jason is a crystal clear reflection of the Gen Y's "can do" attitude and affinity for mentors. He offers valuable perspective for taking charge of your life and working with other generations in a positive manner.

Gen Y Project:

Your path to success took several detours. Could you give us some background on your life?

Jason:

I grew up in a small town with a pretty modest background. I was always the shortest kid in my grade — everything was big in Texas except me! When I finally got to high school, I didn't fit in and ended up hanging out with a lot of young people who didn't make the best choices. The irony in most public schools is that the most accepting group is often the troublemakers because they don't care how you look or dress as long as you get into trouble with them.

So, I was hanging out with these troublemakers when my tenth grade science teacher, Mr. Price, pulled me aside and said I needed to get serious about my future. He said if I didn't, I was going to end up like my friends, which was a dead-end street. When Mr. Price reached out to me, he changed my life. He asked me what I wanted to do when I grew up. I told him I wanted to be a doctor, so he encouraged me to apply to a summer medical program in Florida where I could get on a plane, leave Texas, see the world a little bit, and try out a career — all while still in high school.

Mr. Price's belief in me got me to realize that I had nothing to lose by applying for the program, which was a huge leap in mindset for me. I applied and to my total surprise, I got in. I later found out that one of the reasons I was accepted was because I lived in the smallest town of anyone who applied. Basically, my application got extra consideration because I was the most rural.

I went to that summer program and quickly realized that I didn't want to be a doctor. That one early career discovery separated me from a lot of people my age because they didn't try out careers while still in high school — they just kind of went headlong into one direction with this idea of what it's going to be like, but it often isn't. My perspective changed because of that one summer in Florida; I met people from all over the world, survived living in a dorm and taking college classes, and basically, realized for the first time that I could do anything I set my mind to. I came back to school with this new attitude, and Mr. Price asked me the same question again, knowing I no longer wanted to be a doctor.

I told him that I had just watched Indiana Jones and that I now wanted to be an archeologist. Once again, he helped me figure out how to apply for summer archaeology programs. By this point, I knew that the worst they could say is no — and they say it by mail. Now when I speak to young people, I tell them that the biggest secret to getting into a good college, getting a respectable job, or even getting a date is that you have to apply — if you don't, you have no chance of getting what you want. I applied to several archeology programs and was rejected from all of them except one, and it happened to be through Harvard University. So, I left my small town again, this time to live in Israel for three months and work on an archaeological dig. I was the youngest person in the program, and the entire experience was much different than I expected — it was 120 degrees, and I was digging with a toothbrush!

I loved living in a foreign country and studying ancient artifacts and ancient civilizations, but I quickly knew that there was no way I could ever be an archaeologist. I was now 17 years old and had two careers down. I decided to take what I had learned and go to college full time. A

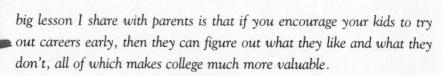

big lesson I share with parents is that if you encourage your kids to try out careers early, then they can figure out what they like and what they don't, all of which makes college much more valuable.

I ended up skipping my senior year of high school and going to a college in New York on full financial assistance. While I was there, part of my financial aid package was to tutor other students. I was assigned to tutor a guy named Tony, who was from New York City. He didn't look like me or talk like me. We could hardly understand each other during that first tutoring session, but by the end of the academic year, his reading was significantly improved, and the experience of working with him completely changed my life.

By helping Tony, I understood for the first time what it meant to help someone in a lasting way. His gratitude for my efforts was overwhelming. After that, I went back to Texas to finish college; I was 18 and, like a lot of college students, thought I had it all figured out. Then a guest came to speak to our class. To my surprise, the guest speaker ended up saying some things that really got to me. The biggest was that if my goal in life was money, I would never have enough because I'd always want more. You don't hear things like that in business school.

Growing up without a lot of money at some key periods in my life, it was easy for me to think that success was all about money and other external things. This speaker was saying that success happened not on the outside but on the inside. His words both irritated and inspired me, so I took the biggest risk of my life and wrote him a letter asking him to be my mentor. After a few conversations, he accepted and became my first formal mentor. He helped me to see — by asking the right questions — that my life mission was not pursuing money in the business world but helping young people from tough backgrounds realize that they could do something positive with their life.

By this time, many of my old friends had given up on themselves and thought that living in a single-wide next to their mama's double-wide was the best they could do. I knew they could do more, and I wanted to prove it, so late one night in 1997, I decided to write a book to help them. I got out of bed and started writing Graduate To Your Perfect Job, *not knowing at all what I was getting into. Three weeks later, I finished the first draft. Then I borrowed money from everyone I knew so I could publish the book myself. I didn't know I couldn't do it, so I kept asking for help until I got what I needed. I ended up turning 19 with $50,000 in debt, 5,000 books, and sleeping on the beige carpet of a friend's garage apartment.*

Gen Y Project:

You hit a low point in your life. How did you come out of it?

Jason:

This was definitely the scariest time of my life, but looking back, I can say I never felt more alive. When word of the book finally started to spread, I was invited to speak at a local school to a group of tough-to-reach students about getting their first job. For whatever reason, the students thought my talk was hilarious. I showed them how to tie a necktie, how to shake hands, and how to let go of their excuses. That one talk led to other speeches. Soon I was speaking at schools and youth conferences almost every single day. A year later, the book really took off, and I started speaking at big conferences for educators. They saw me hold the attention of their toughest students and asked, "Can you teach us how you get through to them? You don't look or talk like them, but they listen to you."

After a few years, I went from speaking to Gen Y and their educators to speaking to their employers and other business leaders. Graduate to Your Perfect Job became a national bestseller and now 1600 schools and colleges use it as a supplementary course. In fact, it's estimated that over 100,000 members of Gen Y have used the book I wrote at age 18 to get their first job or a better job!

Gen Y Project:

That success really speaks to what we've been talking about since we started the Gen Y Project, which is teaching kids essential life skills.

Jason, one of the problems we see with Gen Y is that they have this terrific momentum going into a new job or experience and then seem quickly deflated when it doesn't fulfill their expectations. You had an excellent example in your book My Reality Check Bounced *with a young woman named Tiffany. Can you share your insight on this trend?*

Jason:

I think it's a result of how we grew up. I see it all the time when I speak at corporations. A young professional will pull me aside after my talk and say, "I never thought it was going to be like this; what do I do now?" The reality is that most of us were told if we just follow the steps our parents and school counselors outlined to us, we would be successful in no time. This works for a few of us, but for most of us, there are all kinds of unexpected challenges and setbacks and other stuff that happens along the way that we are unprepared to handle.

On top of that, Gen Y has huge expectations and a strong sense of entitlement — we think we're just going to show up to work and quickly get promoted. We're completely focused on the outcome and not the process, and we are not accustomed to paying our dues. Then we get out in the real world and get that first job. It's like Tiffany's case, where she thought it was going to be all perfect until she quickly discovered how hard she had to work, how stressful it was, how her boss didn't treat her the way she thought she should be treated, and how she didn't make the money she dreamed about. It all came crashing down because she'd worked since kindergarten to get to this position as a college graduate with a solid first job, yet it felt hollow.

That's when her reality check bounced, as I call it. You have this vision about where you're going. But when you get there, instead of being CEO at 27, you're sharing a cubicle with three people (one who doesn't shower), you're working across from the bathroom, and you're having to do tasks that you wouldn't ask your baby brother to do. Then, you wonder, "Is this it? What do I do now?" Many of us do not know what to do next. That's when we move back home if we'd moved out, use credit card balance transfers to sustain our lifestyle, make short-term decisions, and flounder around as opposed to trying to figure out what's going to make us happy. The tough wake-up call is when you eventually realize that the paths that make you financially rich or give you a big title may not ultimately make you happy. That's just hard for us to accept, so we instead stay on paths that are not fulfilling because they are safe. The key first step to breaking free of this unfulfilling path is recognizing that no matter how trapped, lost, or frustrated you feel, you are not stuck. You have the power to choose what you do and where you go every day.

And the flip side to all this is that our mom and dad told us that as long as we're in school, they'll keep paying some of our bills, so we creatively postpone graduation and negotiate to stay on their car insurance as long as possible. I've even seen it get so bad that parents fill out job applications for their adult kids! I know parents are simply trying to make it easier for their kids than it was for them, but when you keep saving grown children, you make them more dependent by taking away the painful life lessons that ultimately makes them stronger, wiser, and more self-reliant.

And then when a young person who has been given everything gets into the real world, they respond very differently to challenges and setbacks than somebody who has struggled on their way up.

I recently spoke at a big workforce conference where I heard about this directly from employers who said to me after my talk, "You're right that your generation feels entitled. They want all this stuff now, and yet they don't even know what they should do to get promoted. They think they can do the minimum and get a big reward for their lack of effort." The reality is that many of us in Gen Y have never been told what it takes to go out

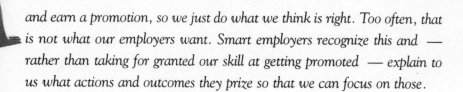

and earn a promotion, so we just do what we think is right. Too often, that is not what our employers want. Smart employers recognize this and — rather than taking for granted our skill at getting promoted — explain to us what actions and outcomes they prize so that we can focus on those.

Gen Y Project:

I have to always remind people that this generation didn't get where they are alone. They had help from parents who contributed to this sense of entitlement.

Jason:

They definitely had help, but it was with the best of intentions. It's not like Baby Boomer parents want their kids to be weak and dependent — quite the opposite. They want them to be super successful and think that by making their life easier, they are putting their kids on the fast track to long-term success. But the Baby Boomers who consistently save their kids from consequences when they should be treating them as adults are the same parents who approach me after a conference and say, "My son is 28 years old. He finally got his bachelor's. How do I get him out of the house?" It's simple — change the locks!

Gen Y Project:

We've empowered them with these dependency traits and now we're paying for this indulgence.

Jason:

You're absolutely right. For example, if we don't like a job, we quit and don't feel guilty about it. We've never in our lives expected to work for one employer for forty years; we knew we were going to be changing jobs maybe even start our own business some day. Where I live, if you work for a company and aren't promoted every year, you quit because your career has stalled. That's difficult for traditional employers to understand. The challenge for traditional employers is realizing that Gen Y has the ability to perform at the high level employers want, but employers have to manage us differently to get the results they're looking for. Our priorities and workplace perspective are different based on how we were raised and what we experienced growing up.

Gen Y Project:

Silent Generation leaders expect a certain approach, Baby Boomers expect a certain approach, Gen Xers expect a certain approach, and Gen Y is no different. Every generation comes with its own communication style, its own culture, and its own way of viewing the world. I would say that is why they're listening to you and not their teachers — you know how to communicate with them.

Jason:

It's just making the effort to look at the world through their lens. People tend to fall back on stereotypes, but if you take a moment to get through that and look at the different priorities, it's a lot easier to figure out how to lead Gen Y. But it does take time and confidence to be open to different viewpoints — especially those different from your own. Smart employers are going to try to make work fun, interesting, and meaningful for Gen Y. Otherwise, if all you're offering is a job and a paycheck, there are ten other companies offering the same thing. As soon as one of them offers your Gen Y employees more money, they will leave with little regret because you've given them no extra incentive to stay.

If you're interested in hiring and keeping Gen Y, you should know that, as a whole, money is not enough to keep them around unconditionally. Gen Y wants to feel an emotional connection to the company's leaders, mission, and culture — all of which can be done without paying them a dollar more in salary.

Gen Y Project:

Gen Y wants work that's meaningful. They want to be challenged, they want a fun environment, they want flexibility, and they want to have camaraderie with their colleagues. With some of their older colleagues, you can dangle money at them and they'll say, "Okay, I'll stay." But that doesn't seem to enter into the Gen Y thought process. It might for the moment, but it won't keep them there.

Jason:

Not long-term — and long-term is different to us anyway. Long-term to us might be two years, but to other generations it might be five or ten years or maybe more. Rather than going in with the expectation that if we do a good job, we can get promoted within three years, we go in with the expectation that if we do a good job now, then we want to be promoted now. If you're not willing to promote me, then I'll go somewhere else where they will. That sense of instant gratification and tangible progress is critically important to us. Our peer group sees nothing wrong with changing jobs every six months — especially if you're bored at work.

Gen Y Project:

Some major corporations are saying that they're having a tough time keeping young leaders. The belief that working one year doesn't look good on a resume simply doesn't compute with them.

Jason:

As long as somebody else will hire them — and the worst side effect of being unemployed is moving home for a little while — Gen Y will keep trying new jobs and companies until they find the one that fits.

Gen Y Project:

I have read that getting your child to apply for a student loan and helping pay that off, even if you can afford the tuition, makes them realize how much money it costs to invest in their future.

Jason:

Anything parents can do to reinforce personal financial accountability is good for Gen Y's growth. Supposedly, we're the most affluent generation ever. There's always been a lot of money around us, and we want what it can buy, but too many of us do not realize the effort that goes into making that kind of money — and that just having money doesn't guarantee happiness. We have to find the right balance between being responsible and having a life. Forcing us to pay our own bills, especially after age 18, is a great step in the right direction.

One thing I want to be sure to mention is that many times when Gen Y is discussed, people focus on the Gen Yers who are going to or went to college. Maybe on a good day, 50 percent of the Gen Yers who start high school actually graduate from college — and that varies dramatically based on where you live. One school where I spoke earlier this week told me their graduating class had the second highest graduation rate in that part of the entire state, and that rate was 70 percent. The lowest in their region had a 55 percent graduation rate.

If you look at the longitudinal data of students who graduate high school and enroll in college, many of them simply don't finish. So we have to be careful when we talk about Gen Y that we don't just talk about those who graduate college because we would be overlooking millions of young adults.

Gen Y Project:

College is not for every young person. I've talked to so many twenty-something leaders who either chose to go to college later or didn't go at all, and they are doing extremely well.

Jason, you talk a little bit in chapter two of your book about a young man named Jimmy getting a mentor, and you also did that. We've heard from several of our twenty-something experts that they sought a mentor. What is it about this generation that makes them want to have a mentor in their life?

Jason:

From my own experience of having divorced parents, I can say that I really wanted a strong male role model consistently in my life that could help me move forward. For whatever reason, the guy who was our guest speaker in college really connected with me. Most people I speak to who are my age confide that they want a coach or mentor in their life — somebody that's on their side without an agenda — but the scary part is asking somebody to accept that role.

In my view, the key to getting a mentor is to get clear on what you want from them. For example, I now have about six different mentors, and they all help me in different life areas. Each one is good at something specific, and that's the area we focus on. When looking for a mentor, you might ask yourself: Do you just want someone to talk to? Do you want someone who can help you advance your career? Do you want someone who can help you start your own business? Do you want someone to teach you how to live your life with more balance or passion? Once you figure that out, it's much easier to find the right mentor.

The hard part is then asking them to be your mentor. If you're nervous about this, just remember that the worst they can say is no. And if that happens, it just means they're not the right one for you. The clearer you are about what you want from your mentor, the faster you will find them. I often share that I have discovered my mentors at places such as a restaurant or the post office, or by seeing them on television, or by sending them an unsolicited Email or cold-calling them. The secret is that when I meet or hear about someone who might be a good mentor, I take the risk to ask. You just have to be brave enough to ask.

When someone does agree to be your mentor, it's important to set clear expectations early so they're not leery about your intentions. I found it's extremely helpful to say, "Here's what I'm expecting. Does that work for you?"

Gen Y Project:

What you're talking about is a great life skill. People are willing to help if they know your intentions are genuine.

Jason:

I've found that people, especially successful people, are extremely willing to help if they feel you are going to value their time and act on their suggestions. My mentors have introduced me to the president of the United States, invested their personal money to help me start a new business, and opened all kinds of other doors that have proved invaluable.

I also think that Gen Y can learn a great deal from people their own age if they create room for dialogue about the issues that are important to them. For me, I helped start a "Go and Grow" group with six people who are within five years of my age. Each of these six people owns their own businesses and has reached a certain level of success. We get together for three hours once a month and talk about what's going on in our lives and with our work, and what challenges we're facing. Most of all, we make it safe to ask for help. In this group, we really strive to be a resource for each other. The advice we need might be a recommendation for a realtor or web designer, or we might simply give candid thoughts on healthy relationships. Being a part of this group is one of the greatest

243 «

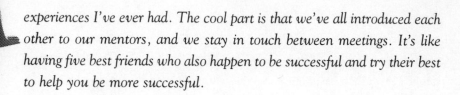

experiences I've ever had. The cool part is that we've all introduced each other to our mentors, and we stay in touch between meetings. It's like having five best friends who also happen to be successful and try their best to help you be more successful.

Gen Y Project:

Jason, in your book, you talk about another life skill: checking your excuses at the door. Is that something you address with your Gen Y groups?

Jason:

I talk about that every time I speak to groups of Gen Y at colleges, schools, and companies. Sometimes I even have participants compete to see who has the best excuse! While this is funny, I use this as a starting point to talk about how prevalent excuses are within our generation. I want people to see that excuses keep us from taking the risks and responsibility we need to get ahead fast.

At a recent government-sponsored event, I asked the participants which excuses they hear the most from Gen Y. The number one answer was not having enough money. The interesting part was there were many personal stories of people in the room who had started with no money but were able to succeed. The obvious conclusion was that when someone says they can't be successful because they don't have enough money, what they're really saying is they don't want their dreams badly enough to make them happen. If they wanted them badly enough, they would find an ethical way to overcome their financial situation and get their degree, start their own business, or land that job they really want.

Gen Y Project:

Can you offer any words of wisdom to Gen Y and the people who are trying to help them grow?

Jason:

I don't know if it's wisdom, but a parting observation is that as parents and employers and members of Gen Y, I think the more we have this kind of open dialogue, the better it's going to be for all of us. We need to work together so we can benefit from our collective strengths.

POINTS FOR REFLECTION

 The biggest secret to landing a great internship, getting accepted to a selective college, securing a loan to start your own business, or acquiring your dream job is taking the risk to apply. If you don't apply, you have no chance of getting in. Sometimes you may have to apply multiple times to get in, but if you don't give up, you will eventually get the opportunity you desire.

 Get a head start on success by exploring careers early and shadowing professionals to see what you like or dislike about each career and company. If you start early (in high school or even middle school), your college and early adult decisions will be easier and much more rewarding because of the perspective and experience you've gained.

 If making money is your only goal in life, you will never be satisfied, because you will always want more. It is important to value life's intangibles (e.g., helping, teaching, volunteer work, social causes) to see what really ignites your passion. That's where the real juice in life comes from.

 Take the time to look closely at the questions you have about your life and career path. Then, ask someone whom you respect to mentor you around your personal and professional goals — and don't be afraid to ask for help. The worst they

can say is no. The majority of experienced professionals love to give advice to young people, so you are actually giving them a huge compliment by asking for their advice.

 Check your excuses at the door. Each time you make an excuse, you avoid taking responsibility for your actions and ultimately, that refusal either sabotages or delays the growth and experiences you need for success.

ABOUT JASON DORSEY

An energetic, insightful, dynamic young leader, **Jason Dorsey** is a sought-after speaker, author, and entrepreneur. His newest book is titled *My Reality Check Bounced!* Only 29, Jason has already been featured on 20/20, NBC's Today Show, ABC's The View, and in *Fortune Magazine, USA Today,* and *The Wall Street Journal.* You can learn more about Jason at <u>www.JasonDorsey.com</u>.

» CHAPTER 21 «

San Francisco International Airport: Michelle DiPilla

"They can face challenges and show the ability to rise above the situation, join together as a community, and get ready for what's to come."

Gen Y has grown up in a different world than those generations who came before. They take technology for granted because it has always existed in their lives. They have been infused with self-esteem by the Baby Boomer parents who wanted to give them more than they had. And they have the ability to start their own businesses — and move home if it doesn't work out.

Along the road to maturity, however, Gen Y hasn't had the chance to develop essential life skills that will help them integrate into a multi-generational society. Their communication methods of email and texting differ from the preferred face to face contact of older generations. They don't understand time management, and they lack the ability to stand in front of a living, breathing group of real people because their world exists so much in a virtual mode.

The San Francisco International Airport has a highly successful internship program that is helping young people develop these workplace skills. The interns range from high achieving college students to at-risk young people, but the two groups share a common need for real world training. Michelle DiPilla heads the SFO

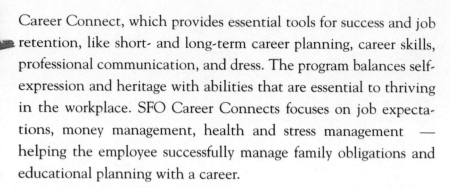

Career Connect, which provides essential tools for success and job retention, like short- and long-term career planning, career skills, professional communication, and dress. The program balances self-expression and heritage with abilities that are essential to thriving in the workplace. SFO Career Connects focuses on job expectations, money management, health and stress management — helping the employee successfully manage family obligations and educational planning with a career.

Michelle understands the importance of mentoring young people, particularly those who have more significant life challenges. Her program's well-rounded approach creates a valuable corps of employees from a source that might not be considered worth the effort by other organizations.

Gen Y Project:

Michelle, what is the SFO Career Connect and how does it help Gen Y develop in the workplace?

Michelle:

The airport has had a commitment to internships for quite a while now; we have seven that vary from high school to the post-graduate level. These programs, usually three months in length, meet our commitment to the surrounding communities and prepare the Gen Y workforce.

SFO Career Connect provides at-risk youth between 18 and 25 with an internship that's beyond our normal three-month stint. The program provides support, structure, skill building, and a coaching model that youth can use for the long-term. This meets the city's commitment to workforce development, and it's an outstanding way to develop our current young people into future leaders.

Gen Y Project:

How does SFO Career Connect work?

Michelle:

We recruit community organizations that work with at-risk youth, so the agencies we partner with have different specialties. Some work with interns that were formerly in foster care, some work with the homeless population, and others work with neighborhoods that may be facing economic challenges.

Gen Y Project:

How do you define "at-risk" youth?

Michelle:

At SFO, it is a young person who, despite having faced personal challenges like foster care or young parenthood, is committed to succeeding and developing a plan of action.

Gen Y Project:

What kind of training is involved?

Michelle:

The 10 interns we select are completing an intense, one-week training that covers airport protocol and interpersonal communication; it also features an intern alumna presentation. We have our past interns come back and talk about their successful experience because peer support is essential.

We also provide a career dress appointment. The airport is a formal business structure, so they go through the entire process of adapting and

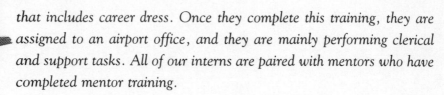

that includes career dress. Once they complete this training, they are assigned to an airport office, and they are mainly performing clerical and support tasks. All of our interns are paired with mentors who have completed mentor training.

The mentor training covers an overview of Gen Y traits and the different ways that mentors can help our interns improve their self-esteem. During the three months they're with the program, the interns continue to receive support from our office, such as transportation vouchers, and they meet with our intern team leader, who is a college undergraduate. We also continue to partner with our agencies and cover topics like money management and balancing family obligations.

So, while interns are in this process of meeting their commitment, their goal is to make it to graduation. In order to graduate, our interns have to show that they can be on time and on schedule, and that they can come to work with a positive attitude. In our last four sessions, nine out of the ten interns graduated in each session. We're really proud of that because there are a lot of issues both at work and outside of work that our interns are managing to be able to make it to graduation.

Gen Y Project:

What happens after the interns graduate from the program? Is there a continued relationship or support system?

Michelle:

The graduation is not the final part of SFO Career Connect, which is what makes this unique. What we wanted to do is really develop our youth. We make the graduation part two of their experience. They continue meeting with our office, training, attending job fairs, and participating in one-on-one coaching. Based on this, we have been able to reach 100 percent transition to permanent employment in our last two sessions.

Gen Y Project:

This is outstanding given their life constraints and the situations they're facing. Michelle, I understand that a large number of your interns are working with men and women from the Silent Generation, many of whom are as old as their grandparents. How successful are these relationships when the generational gap is so great?

Michelle:

We've also seen something interesting with the mentors that are in the Traditionalist or Silent Generation. Many of our SFO Career Connect interns have been raised by their grandparents, so we've seen our Gen Yers connect quite well to the Traditionalists and Baby Boomers. Even though this generation is well developed, that need for self-esteem is still there.

Our Gen Y interns really want to hear how they're doing and we've implemented a performance appraisal system that's a little different from our city bureaucratic evaluation. It allows for the intern to develop skill building and talk about a lot of other things. Sometimes they're talking in-depth about personal issues they're facing, and a lot of our mentors are taken aback — they say they don't know how to handle this.

From the Gen Y perspective, they're wondering what's wrong with talking about every aspect of their life, so we've included that in our personal performance appraisal — it's great to share, but balance needs to be met.

Gen Y Project:

What shifts have you noticed in the Traditionalists now that they are mentoring Gen Y?

Michelle:

Traditionalists are slowly becoming more comfortable with the fact that they can still check their interns' work without hovering over them, and

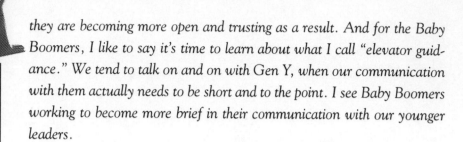

they are becoming more open and trusting as a result. And for the Baby Boomers, I like to say it's time to learn about what I call "elevator guidance." We tend to talk on and on with Gen Y, when our communication with them actually needs to be short and to the point. I see Baby Boomers working to become more brief in their communication with our younger leaders.

Gen Y Project:

A lot of corporate leaders are saying that Gen Y tends to think nothing of discussing personal matters at work and then, when they're reprimanded, they break down in tears and start to talk even more to their older colleagues about their problems. How do we find that balance and help Gen Y understand there's a time and a place for this type of emotional response?

Michelle:

We have our office act as the middle point between the intern and the supervisor. This lets the intern know that if they have issues, they should come to us. This allows Gen Y to be straightforward, and we're prepared that there may be some emotional things going on, and they feel comfortable in having us be their spokesperson. When they're with their mentor, we've let them know they need to keep it a little more professional, and that means keeping some of those personal, more emotional things aside while they are on the job.

Gen Y Project:

How does Gen Y feel about performance appraisals? Are they receptive?

Michelle:

Sometimes there's the belief that Gen Y knows everything. We've noted that Gen Y responds in a positive way to feedback, and what helps is a mode to give the feedback. Having an informal monthly performance appraisal is really beneficial to the Gen Y intern. We've also found that providing positive feedback — even just the basic "you're on the right track" — is important to them. Also, they need to be given clear instruction, and that's something we found some difficulty with initially, but we keep working with our interns until we make sure we get through to them.

We once had a mentor providing instruction, and we noticed that the intern was in need of a little more detail. We've found that feedback and instructions really need to be given in steps…1, 2, 3 — that's how the interns want to hear it. That has helped immensely with getting projects done, and it has allowed them to feel that they're really in control and successful in accomplishing something.

They also want to feel that there's respect for who they are, which includes meeting family obligations. They want to know if they need time off for a medical appointment for their child, that's available to them. At the same time, they know that they need to stay on top of documentation such as a "time off" form — a little more structure for them — and with instruction and support, they do adapt to this structure.

Gen Y Project:

When you say that you have a monthly informal appraisal, tell us what feedback you provide and what skill sets or proficiency you measure.

Michelle:

One of the resources we've used to develop our appraisal is from Developing Self-Esteem *by Connie Palladino, and I really recommend it. Connie talks about the things we're all familiar with such as technical skills, volume of work, and so on, but she's added some things that were beneficial to us — initiative, planning, and presentation skills.*

We've also found that a lot of times interns have a little difficulty adapting to the workplace, especially when it comes to communications and

giving presentation. It's important for us as mentor and coaches to work with Gen Y and develop their confidence to speak in front of a group as well as with different levels of management.

Gen Y Project:

You talk about both high achieving and at-risk interns. These groups seem to be coming from different perspectives. How do you relate the two?

Michelle:

Most of the high-achieving interns we have are college interns that are applying from universities all across the country. Although it's a separate program from SFO Career Connect, we have found we're seeing some similar traits with our mentors and coaches.

I define a "high achieving intern" as somebody who's participated in extracurricular activities at school, is in the AP classes, and is getting above a 4.0. I can give an example of one of our of high school interns. She's going to one of the University of California campuses this fall, and she has above a 4.0 average and so many units that she's definitely meeting her graduation date early. Then, our at-risk interns who have just graduated or completed a GED have little work experience, have not participated in a lot of extracurricular activities, and are facing other issues like young parenthood or foster care.

Gen Y Project:

How are these young men and women responding to some of these bigger life skills? I know Gen Y spends a lot of time online and text messaging. How do they respond when you talk about spending time with developing their presentation skills?

Michelle:

Well, the first response is one of fear. Gen Y is definitely used to being on the phone or behind the computer monitor. At the same time, once that fear settles down and they know there's going to be instruction and practice, they respond positively. With something like presentation skills, there needs to be some type of support from the mentor/supervisor.

Gen Y Project:

What would you say has made this program so successful?

Michelle:

First, I feel we have created a program that fits Gen Y's values, and that's won the support of the interns. For example, this program provides career exposure, skill development, and some financial support, which can help with their schooling and other responsibilities. The second thing that's been essential is proving that interns are accepted for who they are, but they're also held accountable.

Lastly, SFO Career Connect has done a great job with developing strategic partnerships, which come in two ways. One is the community, such as agencies or schools, and the second is in-house. There needs to be commitment by staff to mentor interns. What's exciting about this experience is that it's a great way to develop an employee's leadership skills and make them into a coach. This is an opportunity for employers and educators to learn about Gen Y and get them ready for the new workforce.

Gen Y Project:

You have a great graduation rate. I'm sure you've had some interns that have said, "I don't think I'm going to make it." How do you get them to stick it out and get the full reward of the experience?

Michelle:

We've had that happen. We try to be flexible, changing the work schedule if necessary; that's the first thing we assess. That allows them to deal with childcare and transportation — a revised schedule will often allow an intern to make it to graduation. We've also seen the need to change work assignments to match jobs with skill levels when we see the work is at a higher level than the intern's skills; plus we provide the intern with more training so that they can perform at a higher level.

We've also seen issues around money management and made that a required portion of this program. Money management seems like a basic issue, but a lot of intern's are forced to pay rent. If they don't pay the rent, it's hard for them to complete the program because they will lose their housing — and many of our interns don't have family support if they can't make their rent payment. Making money management part of this program not only makes sure their housing situation is okay, but it gives them a sense of control.

Gen Y Project:

Besides the money skills, what other areas do you see where mentors might be able to fill in the blanks?

Michelle:

Around personal issues, a lot of it has to do with listening skills. One of the things we've really advised Gen Y to do is not be embarrassed to take notes. Some things are not available to them at the touch of a button, so we've developed ways for them to work with their listening skills, as well as their planning and time management skills.

Gen Y Project:

Is there anything else that can be taught across the whole to help them excel?

Michelle:

One thing is interpersonal communication. We've noticed the varying written skill sets; this has been a big concern for the mentors. We're encouraging many of our interns to go back to school and develop their writing skills. We encourage the mentors to let them feel that failure is okay sometimes and can actually strengthen them both personally and professionally. The Gen Yers that we're seeing are consistently dropping from classes, and we have our mentors encouraging them to stick it out and see what the results are.

Gen Y Project:

It seems like giving up and moving on is the norm for this group — that they need flexibility to do and go as it suits them. Are you finding that?

Michelle:

Absolutely. We are part of a city structure with a lot of rules, and even we are looking at flexible schedules, telecommuting, and so on. A lot of other companies and industries are adapting to this need for flexibility — we really want to meet the needs of our employees because that will ultimately make us more successful.

Gen Y Project:

In an airport that operates 24/7, you really need to rely on your employees showing up. Does Gen Y's need for flexibility cause concern for you?

Michelle:

Even though there is flexibility, there is also a sense of commitment to make sure that things are covered. We encourage our interns to realize that because we are a 24-hour operation, showing up to work is very important.

Gen Y Project:

What leadership traits do you see Gen Y bringing to the table?

Michelle:

The one that's really at the forefront for me is their ability to adapt. We're seeing an interest in achieving personal success, and part of that is having career success, which comes from having a goal-minded attitude. I think Gen Y does have this attitude and we're helping those who are weak in this regard to develop it in all elements of life. We require our interns to have a goal calendar every day, and it doesn't have to be strictly work related. Achievements in your personal life, whether financial or in a living situation, are essential to development.

They also have perseverance that's incredible. This generation has had so many things being thrown at them, and they've seen so many things thrown at us as a nation that they have the ability to face challenges and show the ability to rise above the situation, join together as a community, and get ready for what's to come. I learn from them every day.

Gen Y Project:

Based on what you're seeing, how do you think Gen Y is going to be leading others in the future?

Michelle:

What I'm most impressed by is the ability for peers to motivate each other. That is essential and I think it will continue to take place. Together, they will be changing norms because they are developing a true sense of community and camaraderie.

POINTS FOR REFLECTION

Two of the key skills employers are asking Generation Y to improve are professional interpersonal and presentation skills. These guidelines will support you in strengthening your skill set:

 As a Generation Yer you are most likely very comfortable with email, instant messaging, and text messaging. But how comfortable and confident are you with face to face communications? Assess your comfort level and talk with a mentor or coach who can help you develop strategies for increasing your confidence during live interactions.

 Work on the basics: dressing professionally, smiling, shaking hands, making eye contact, and meeting and greeting people with a warm, confident presence will go a long way in the business world. The best way to improve in these areas is to practice in front of a mirror or converse with friends and family, and ask for the feedback. Start out by practicing a 30-second introduction, and move on to a one-minute spiel on your favorite YouTube video or a current event.

 Take up a hobby or volunteer position that is focused on mingling. Try tutoring, reading to the blind, or facilitating a book club discussion. The more you interact with people, the more confident you will become in your face to face communications.

 Interview ten professionals about their career and/or company, and schedule these interviews to take place in person. Write out your questions in advance and use this time to practice asking powerful questions and really listening to their answers — listening is a huge part of professional interactions.

 Ask ten friends to interview you on ten different subjects and record the interviews. Listen to the recordings, and perform a self-critique (make sure these interviews are conducted face to face). These subjects can be on anything from cooking to biking to your latest vacation. Each time you conduct your next interview, practice refining your skill set.

ABOUT MICHELLE DIPILLA

Michelle DiPilla is the SFO and Training Programs Coordinator for the San Francisco International Airport. Michelle has received special recognition for her work with SFO Career Connect, a program for at-risk youth from ages 18 to 24 who have faced personal challenges but are motivated to find career and personal focus.

» CHAPTER 22 «

People and Organization Development Group: Michael Berger

"This situation feels like a diversity issue. It's really about noticing that people are different. There's not a right or wrong, but just different ways of looking at things."

Gen Y is growing up and spreading out. They are streaming into the workforce and bringing with them a tide of change. With their unique behaviors and attitudes, they are churning up new issues in the workplace. And many Gen Yers are being held afloat by hovering parents who make waves while trying to do what they see as best for their grown children.

This phenomenon is reaching massive proportions in the United States, but what about the rest of the world? We often hear that rapid technological advances have flattened the world and created a global community. Is the Gen Y influence the same in other countries?

Michael Berger, an executive coach from America, has international expertise on this issue. He works with organizations on working across generations to create a harmonious, productive environment. Michael is currently living in New Zealand, where he is one of the principal advisers with the People and Organization Development Group with the New Zealand Department of

Conservation. He has clients in several countries, and he has gathered first-hand information on Gen Y in and out of the U.S.

Gen Y Project:

How does an American coach end up in New Zealand?

Michael:

Essentially, it was about having an opportunity to follow up on the work that I had been doing around generational and leadership issues. For the past couple of years, I've been tackling the issue of dealing with the demographic shift that is taking place around the world with the different generations. I've focused on working within organizations and across the private sector, public sector, for-profit, and non-profit, covering a range of industries.

Before I moved to New Zealand, I had been living in New York and Washington, D.C. I discovered that organizations were interested in taking more tangible actions toward understanding generational demographics. They were learning about the developing leadership vacuum and turnover rates, especially among younger people.

I found that, while there was some interest, there still was a fair amount of apprehension to delve into this new domain, which surprised me. They were feeling the effect from what was happening and doing a little bit of projecting to say, "This is something we really have to pay attention to."

Around the same time, my wife, who is a university professor and does a lot of work in leadership on her own, became involved in overseas work and noticed different attitudes in other countries on some of these same issues. She started consulting for a colleague in New Zealand, working in Australia and with some government agencies in New Zealand. She became most interested in working with her colleague and, she had six months sabbatical coming up, so we decided to try New Zealand for a while. As an independent consultant, I had a fair amount of flexibility.

I had a couple of networking meetings and informational interviews to see if anybody was even interested about generational matters in this part of the world, and I was overwhelmed at the reception about the idea of addressing generational differences. I found an incredible amount of appetite for what I'm doing.

Gen Y Project:

How did you connect with your current job working for the New Zealand government?

Michael:

That informal interview process led to an offer with the Department of Conservation, one of the most important government agencies in New Zealand. There I play a key role in working with the entire organization — from the chief executive down to 23-year-old field and park rangers. I'm working with issues around leadership, generational shifts, and succession planning in a way that is more engaged and receptive than any organization I've come across in anywhere in North America.

Gen Y Project:

So, is this interest in the generational workplace dynamic something that's growing on an international scale?

Michael:

Absolutely! About three months before I left the U.S., I began delivering presentations to multinational firms who have companies in Canada and people in Australia and the U.S. They were facing a similar issue to the U.S. but with a much smaller population.

Gen Y Project:

Are you seeing differences in these other countries from the generational situation in the U.S.?

Michael:

Outside the U.S. borders, it looks and feels a bit different. Certainly, places that have operations in Asia and Western Europe have demographics that are fairly global. There are some differences in other countries, but we're all facing these same issues. What's interesting to me is they're coming up in fairly similar ways, even in diverse cultures.

Gen Y Project:

We always think this issue exists just in our own backyards, but it's much broader.

Michael, you've written about a common trend for older generations to want the Generation Y young leaders to act like them. I also hear the flip side — that Gen Y wants their elders to be more open-minded and flexible. How do we navigate this mutual, but conflicting, desire for others to come around to their particular way of thinking?

Michael:

It's a complicated issue in some respects and, at the same time, easy to distill. In some ways, this situation feels like a diversity issue. It's really about noticing that people are different. There's not a right or wrong, but just different ways of looking at things. So, wanting people to be like you isn't reasonable because people are the way they are and that's it. That's not an excuse to say, "Well, you're different and I'm different, so that's fine." It's not that simple. The issue is about seeing the fact that there are these different ways, and to really effectively work together, we have to figure out how to bridge those differences.

Gen Y Project:

Getting people to see a cultural norm so different from their own is a lot easier said than done.

Michael:

I definitely agree. Developing some supports and structure to help leaders see and hold onto a different perspective is one of the most powerful steps. However, the generational gap is a bit different when it comes to looking at other views because it's not as static. We're not going to have a significant shift in the demographic around men and women in the workplace, personality styles, or ethnicity, but the demographics are rapidly shifting about the generational distribution in the workforce.

Gen Y Project:

What problem is this particular demographic shift causing that the diversity shifts did not?

Michael:

You have power dynamics that come with people in different age groups. Push things one way, and those demographics shift — causing the power dynamics to shift as well. The Boomer way of seeing the world is going to rub up against the increasing numbers of Gen Ys in organizations and create a tension that hasn't existed with so many of these other different groups in the workforce.

Gen Y Project:

What do you envision happening as a result of this tension?

Michael:

I think that is a very big problem. Historically, we have some good examples of what happens when that comes to pass. In the late 60s and early 70s, the Boomers were coming of age and moving into the minority group demographically, working against the established veterans who had been the drivers of cultural and social norms up to that point. Those groups came together and saw some things that they didn't agree on collide with each other, which created a fair amount of friction. Eventually, the Boomers became big enough that they were able to rewrite all of the social values that we hold as true today.

Gen Y Project:

Gen Y is coming in with such a unique perspective, but they are the products of the Baby Boomers who created their own cultural shift 40 years ago.

Michael:

It's absolutely true. One of the knocks on this generation is that they've been so coddled and have had people telling them how much they can accomplish — and they believe it. They have this sense of entitlement. In spite of all the complaints from people who said, "Oh, they're not doing the hard work, they're being taken care of, and they can't fight their own battles," they'll figure out that they still can accomplish what they want — whether it's through support of their parents or others, by using technology, or from the unbelievably broad, fast, and sweeping networks that they can create.

Gen Y Project:

We're talking about an age group that is currently comprised mainly of 18- to 28-year-olds. In about five years, they should all be among the workforce. So what do you think the work landscape will look like in the near future?

Michael:

There are a couple of variables that are a bit hard to account for. By 2012, about 30 percent of the workforce is going to be Gen Y. About the same number — and maybe even a little bit less — are going to be Gen Xers. Boomers will still be about 35 to 40 percent of the workforce, as predictions are that many more people will work beyond 65. They're not going to go away as quietly or as quickly as some of the models suggest.

Either way, if you just look at the numbers, Boomers are only going to represent maybe one-third of the total working population. So a clear majority are going to be either Gen Xers or Gen Yers. There's absolutely some impact there.

How much Gen Y is going to shift the workforce is one of the real uncertainties. I can imagine two different scenarios. One of them is a gentler shift, where the aging Boomers are remembering some of the reasons for their desires 25 years ago. They will see Gen Y as a way to further some of their own goals and beliefs that reflect back to those earlier values when they were growing up.

The other scenario is that this gentle transition doesn't happen. The Gen Yers' force and demands will be such that they're going to start their own organizations or put so much pressure on a few key people as to quickly change the leadership dynamics and the power structure within existing organizations.

So, you have one force coming up against this opposing force of the younger generation where people aren't going to play the game by the same rules or for the same reasons. They're not going to wait their turn in line so they can get the big rewards and the corner office. They want to have impact right now or they're going to leave.

Gen Y Project:

That brings up a good point because many older leaders complain that they're having a hard time keeping younger leaders. The twenty-some-

thing leaders come and go in an instant. Is this something we have to get accustomed to? Are there incentives for retaining these young leaders longer, or is this just the way they are going to lead their lives?

Michael:

I think it is going to require a shift, to a certain degree, in the structure and in the mentality of some of the senior leaders. We're going to be forced to accept that these people aren't going to stay in the same organization for 10, 15, or 20 years. To a stereotypical Gen Xer, six or seven years means three jobs: one independent, one for a small company, and one for a big firm.

The expectation of holding on to these people is a paradigm. It's not one that we can sustain because I see leaders doing the wrong thing to retain people. Trying to restrict these younger people is exactly what they don't want. The way that the older leaders support and sustain business success is counter to what the younger people want to do.

Gen Y Project:

What do these leaders need to do differently in order to keep younger leaders?

Michael:

Across the generations, one of the top reasons people leave jobs is a lack of development — whether it's career, professional, or personal. You'll need to give them opportunities for career or professional development, and make sure that there's training available.

These younger people have a lot of energy, ideas, and mobility. They don't have kids or mortgages yet. It's not that complicated for them to pick up and move to an overseas or a West Coast office for a couple years. From a Boomer's perspective, you just can't pick up your life and move like that for a few years.

Look at the way that the Gen Yers move around, change jobs, move cities, move overseas, live in Europe for a couple years, go to Louisiana for a year and do work there, or go to Africa. This is just part of what makes their life interesting.

Gen Y Project:

Michael, you had mentioned that reverse mentoring environments seem to be working well. What are the keys for an organization to take advantage of this type of relationship in the workplace?

Michael:

Reverse mentoring is a really important resource that people have without even realizing it in many cases. One of the keys is finding people who are eager to be in that relationship on both sides. You need to be clear about what the relationship between the mentor and the mentee is going to look and feel like. Sometimes, the older one will have the expertise; other times, that will be the role of the younger person. I've worked in organizations where people are thrown into these mentoring relationships. They haven't taken the time to structure it. Without the right tools and resources, you think you're right all the time and you don't have to listen to somebody else.

Gen Y Project:

No one likes to be told what to do, especially against their will.

Michael:

Yes, and especially if the person who's telling you what to do is 20 years your junior. So you need to make sure that the structural and support pieces are in place, and the relationship is made up of willing participants. If you can achieve that, mentoring is certainly going to give them some insight and perspective.

Gen Y Project:

Are you seeing a difference in New Zealand from your experiences in the United States?

Michael:

The New Zealanders know that this is a small country with a small population. They have a "little guy" mentality in the world. And it's very interesting because, coming from the U.S., you never think about that. But what I'm a part of here is a very broad-based initiative that is working with younger people who either have been selected by or identified through community groups, schools, and community leadership groups, or they just volunteered to be a part of a broader dialogue.

New Zealanders know that they can make a difference, and they can do things that are a little bit more out of the box than some other countries just based on size and how they want to see themselves. So there is a receptive audience among business and government leaders to play into this conversation and not tell them how to think or how to behave. They are instead looking to get both broad-based and a very specific perspective about what's important to these young people, what ideas they can bring around group process and technology, doing things in different ways, and working towards different goals than the establishment has been able to see. It's amazing to see the way it works.

And so much of it is based on a genuine desire from both sides of the generational dynamics to be in a conversation because the younger people know that if they have the older people in power on their side, then they're going to accomplish their goals a lot more quickly.

Gen Y Project:

What are some of the skills that are missing from Gen Yers coming into the workforce?

Michael:

They just haven't had the need to develop some fundamentals around interpersonal engagements. Older leaders are saying, "Well, they don't look me in the eye and they don't really know how to communicate." There is an expectation of proper business etiquette with the Boomers and the Silent Generations. But at the same time, the younger people are going to have to exist in this world until it changes a little bit more.

Gen Yers don't have the kind of presentation and speaking skills that a lot of people think you need to have in organizations these days. Instead of faulting them, I look to the older generations to take a bit of responsibility. Senior leaders need to be clear about the behaviors that they want and expect, and then be pushed to ask why that is important. To be clear about those reasons, especially for a generation that isn't just going to take things at face value, they need to be able to articulate that.

Additionally, they need to realize the need to have training or awareness building about these fundamental interpersonal engagement skills. Treat it like any new skill sets that are needed to come into the workplace.

It's very easy to fault younger people for not behaving the right way. And I think we can look at how we've allowed our kids to grow up with television, media, and access; those are their social circles. People breaking off relationships through instant messaging would be completely unacceptable to some older people, but that's just the way it is for some younger people.

Gen Y Project:

Gen Yers are playing by a different set of rules.

Michael:

To expect this group of younger people not to send an instant message or a text message is really a stretch. For that to be unacceptable doesn't make sense.

Gen Y Project:

In the U.S., we have a generation of hovering parents who are making so many decisions for their children that they aren't allowing young people to mature and develop the necessary life skills. Are you seeing this abroad, or is this just more prevalent in our culture?

Michael:

There is a little bit of it in other countries, but it's certainly not a factor in India and Asia. The generational shift that's happening in the emerging markets, especially China and India, is such an unbelievable change that you don't have the same dynamics. Their people are really much more out there on their own in the world.

In New Zealand, the attitude toward protecting, hovering, and facilitating things for your kids is something that hasn't hit yet. But at the same time, I think some of these things are changing. And in the United States, there is an "entitled" perspective in younger people and older people. If you don't get the kind of service that you want or expect, you raise a fuss. If you are not given the right kind of deal on this or that, you talk to the manager.

Kids in the U.S. have seen these things and want to do it for themselves. As good parents, we want to take care of our kids, so we'll just do it for them. It perpetuates this helicopter parent, which is absolutely going to stay in the work force for a while, in my opinion. It started out with the parent in the elementary school, wanting to make sure the child had the right teacher; in middle school and high school, they make sure the child has the right grades. And then at the college admissions, they're going on the admission review and then on job interviews and now performance reviews. On one hand, it shows an incredible commitment to our kids; but on the other hand, we're not helping them develop the sort of skills they need.

Gen Y Project:

What about the entitlement mentality? How has this affected Gen Y as young adults?

Michael:

For younger people to grow up, the notion of fairness and "everybody's a winner and everybody gets a trophy" creates respect and appreciation for lots of different things. But at some point along the way, it will not be fair and there won't be people to advocate for your case — you're just going to be stuck on the short end of the stick sometimes. It will be interesting to see how they deal with it, because it won't be a 12-year-old who's dealing with the situation but a 30-year-old, and the stakes will be greater. At some point, these people will be left on their own, but at the same time, I think a lot of them won't. I can imagine the helicopter parenting element might continue on for a long time as parents might live longer.

Gen Y Project:

So the parental interference could be a problem in the workplace. How are managers tackling that new problem?

Michael:

Leaders and their organizations are taking some serious looks at how to deal with the younger employees and their parents. A lot that gets carried along in the wake of this generation as they emerge into the adult world and the workforce have never been seen before.

Gen Y Project:

Coaching is an effective way to deal with issues like these, but will these young people accept coaches from another generation or will they confuse the relationship with mentoring?

Michael:

There aren't a whole lot of coaches that are young because coaching requires the ability to maintain some distance and perspective on things and not be pulled into other people's stories. We are going to need coaches that are younger or that can really engage with people as opposed to falling into a mentoring role.

An important part of coaching involves looking ahead, but you must have some experience and perspective. It's a matter of building a future that isn't based on as much history and has much foundation of a person's own sense of self.

Working with Gen Y is going to require a lot of coaches to be comfortable with more uncertainty than they probably had with clients who have been working for ten more years.

Gen Y Project:

Do you have any advice for Gen Y and for older leaders interested in bridging the generation gap?

Michael:

For older leaders, start with a real commitment to being curious and open to things that may not look or feel familiar or comfortable.

For the younger people, I think there is a lot of evidence of them getting their way and making things happen the way they want. But I try to help them see that there is more than one way to see things; other people aren't wrong. To dismiss how things have been is not going to help you get where you're going any faster. In fact, if anything, it's going to slow you down.

So it's really about similarly having a little bit of patience and openness. When you can engage people, find common points, and then work towards that — even if you're going at it from different ways or towards different goals — it helps move the process along with much less pain and much greater efficiency. Appreciate the things that have come before you, not to be deferential, but in a way that still acknowledges where other people are coming from to help you get to where you want to be.

POINTS FOR REFLECTION

 People from different generations are not necessarily right or wrong. We have unique perspectives. By recognizing the varying views around us, we will continue to grow, learn, and feed an open mind.

 Learning to interact across generations is not a matter of getting the young to act like the old or getting the old to act like the young. It requires a greater shift to find ways to ease ourselves into networks, communities, and organizations so that we work together in a way that achieves a common mission.

 Your parents, teachers, coaches, and bosses can provide you with the structure and support you need to be successful in the future, but in the end, you need to build that future for yourself. No one else can do that for you, and the sooner you take responsibility for that process, the sooner your future will become your present.

 As a young adult, it is sometimes easier to ask parents and authority figures to make decisions for you. Yet one of the best ways to learn in life is to make tough decisions, to solve problems independently, and then learn from the consequences of those decisions.

 As you journey into adulthood, ask for constructive feedback from your parents, teachers, bosses, and coaches. Then be dedicated to applying that feedback in the direction of your

success. Hearing tough feedback is never easy, but it can help you to solve problems and prevent missteps from escalating to the point where they have a negative impact on your life or career.

ABOUT MICHAEL BERGER

Michael Berger is a young veteran of organizations and an expert in human dynamics, generational matters, and systems and change. His background is a blend of specialized training and success with small and Fortune 100 companies. He holds a master's degree in organization development and an advanced certificate in leadership coaching from Georgetown University. Michael also has extensive training and expertise in adult development, personality and communication styles, emotional intelligence, organizational values, and leadership issues in Gen X/Gen Y. For more information, visit Michael at http://www.bergerblog.com.

» PART FIVE «

Media Makes The Difference

Y

» CHAPTER 23 «

The Glimpse Foundation: Nick Fitzhugh

*"It's important to remember to give back to the
community that helped equip you with that
knowledge, so you can help someone else increase
their own knowledge and understanding."*

There are presently 200,000 American students studying abroad
every year. Each one is gathering knowledge and education
about, and experiences with, different cultures. Until recently, there
was no effective method to connect this vast network.

The Glimpse Foundation was founded by Nick Fitzhugh, who is
a reporter, fiction writer, and entrepreneur. At the time, he was a
freshman at Brown University and had an idea for a new approach
to international journalism. Using the Internet he has developed
an online communication channel where students and Peace Corps
volunteers can share stories about their experiences, and where the
friends and families of these overseas travelers can interact as well.

The Glimpse Foundation uses the Internet to connect people
who might never meet otherwise. This online community brings the
world closer for many people and creates yet another social network
that has become a favored source for Gen Y. Young people who are
interested in studying or volunteering in a foreign locale can connect
with people who are living this experience. They can read the first-
hand narratives for a close-up account of stories from abroad.

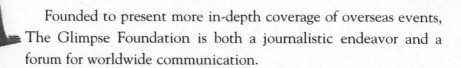

Founded to present more in-depth coverage of overseas events, The Glimpse Foundation is both a journalistic endeavor and a forum for worldwide communication.

Gen Y Project:

Nick, what motivated you to create The Glimpse Foundation?

Nick:

It was officially started in 2001, although the development work began about a year prior. In terms of thinking about the organization's mission, that began considerably earlier — before I even knew it — as I was growing up watching the news with my parents. I was developing an increased understanding for the type of news generally reported within the U.S. and around the world.

As I got a little older and had the opportunity to spend time abroad through an exchange program in high school, I started to see for myself what I had suspected for a long time — that we were just getting a very small piece of the puzzle with regards to news and information about other people, cultures, and countries. For the most part, we just receive news about major events, government proceedings, natural disasters, wars, famines, et cetera.

While that's important and certainly a significant piece of what's going on in the world, it doesn't give people any idea of what a culture is really like — what it would be like to live within it. That creates substantial problems when it comes to foreign policy and trying to understand one another across cultural and national boundaries. When I had a chance to see that for myself, I knew something had to be done about it. My original approach — with my background and interest in fiction writing — was to start writing articles about my experiences abroad.

It was my belief that those types of articles would compel an American audience that is largely disinterested or unaware of the rest of the world, and it worked. The articles I initially wrote were accepted by The Providence Journal, *published, and acclaimed. When I arrived at Brown University as a freshman, I began feeling out interest in my fellow students about these issues.*

From the spring of my freshman year until now, Glimpse has continued to evolve. I had a lot of support from other students; we spent as much time on this project as we did on our other four or five classes combined. I'm not quite sure how we managed to do that, but we did. After college, we worked even longer hours with a smaller staff and we were able to bootstrap the organization to where it is today.

Gen Y Project:

The diligence and rigor with which you pursued this mission reinforces what we're hearing about Gen Y's commitment to making a difference in the world. Yet, in spite of this trend, our young people have a real disconnect with the world outside the boundaries of the United States. I believe I read a report on your website that said approximately 85 percent of Gen Yers cannot identify Afghanistan on a map. What has created this knowledge gap?

Nick:

It is certainly a substantial problem. The statistic is actually courtesy of a National Geographic-Roper poll of 18- to 24-year-olds that was conducted a few years ago.

Also not surprising were the statistics of those who were unable to identify even New Jersey on a map. One reason, which actually has begun to be addressed by news networks, is that maps were not often presented in collaboration with news pieces — lots of photos, footage, and reporting were conveyed, but no maps. With Google maps and other resources,

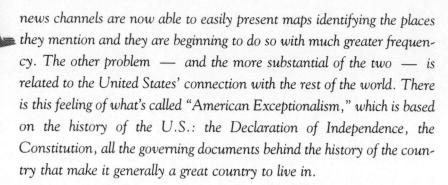

news channels are now able to easily present maps identifying the places they mention and they are beginning to do so with much greater frequency. The other problem — and the more substantial of the two — is related to the United States' connection with the rest of the world. There is this feeling of what's called "American Exceptionalism," which is based on the history of the U.S.: the Declaration of Independence, the Constitution, all the governing documents behind the history of the country that make it generally a great country to live in.

American Exceptionalism is the belief that the United States is sort of a model country and, as U.S. citizens, we can't help but feel a certain sense of privilege or superiority over other people, at least on moral or intellectual grounds. Largely because of this, as a country and within our educational system, we fail to put any emphasis on understanding our connection with the rest of the world.

That connection is something that happens much more often in other countries because of their lack of exceptionalism and because of the size of the country and the number of countries that typically surround them. In Europe, for example, people typically travel between countries much more frequently, so it's a more natural part of daily life to understand their surrounding environments. The U.S. doesn't have that kind of geographic layout, so it's incumbent upon us as individuals and educators to disseminate that information.

Glimpse, among others, is an organization that is working hard to combat the problem, to disseminate geographic knowledge, and to provide a contextual means of sharing stories and establishing connections between individuals. We want to inspire young people to care about the world and provide them with the tools they'll need to better understand it.

Gen Y Project:

What is the benefit for Americans to reach out and know people internationally?

Nick:

The benefits are significant, and they're seen more all the time on different levels and in different ways. On the one hand, an understanding or connection with people in other countries can facilitate business. On the larger level, you have employers in the U.S. and elsewhere who are increasingly looking to hire employees with international experience because of the perceived benefits.

Because of this and the country's increasing recognition of study abroad programs, you are seeing more colleges requiring study abroad for graduation. There is even a congressional effort to fund a program called Abraham Lincoln Fellowships that would get at least one million students studying abroad by 2016, if Congress approves the funding.

One upper level example benefit of having an international perspective, which is one of the underlying foundations for Glimpse, is the degree to which that kind of understanding can broker greater peace and conflict resolution around the world, on a variety of levels within foreign policy that may not even see the light of day.

There are some important lower level advantages, too. It gives you a chance to learn a foreign language. That's great for your resume, but it's also great for your job and your life in general. It gives you an opportunity to live in a completely different environment where you are forced to survive and learn to thrive. That is invaluable as far as individual growth and becoming a strong, more confident person. For most people who spend significant time abroad, it ends up being a very important experience in their lives, for all of these reasons.

Increasingly, there are overseas volunteer or service learning programs that provide opportunities to get involved in helping the communities you're living in. These Peace Corps-esque opportunities also provide another way to enrich your own life while you're enriching the lives of others.

Gen Y Project:

When you start looking at other cultures and how people live their lives, it has a tendency to remove your judgment that your way is right and theirs is wrong. When that type of thinking escalates, people fight over belief systems and cause wars. However, when you look at other cultures, it may actually expand your view of how to do your life a little differently by seeing some of these cultures. This could be a precursor to peace.

Nick:

Just understanding relationships based on mutual, shared experiences and awareness is the most essential and the simplest building block for peace.

The other benefit is the opportunity to make new friends. I can certainly say that that is a fabulous component. For me, spending time abroad and making friends with people from different backgrounds was unbelievably exciting, and I learned so much from it. To this day, one of the largest takeaways for me was how much I could learn from my peers. As a result, I continue to apply that knowledge to my life all the time, and I now have friends all over the world.

Gen Y Project:

Can The Glimpse Foundation help students get started with study abroad?

Nick:

Study abroad is still something that affects a tiny fraction of the population, so we want anyone who has done it to share their experiences to impact and improve the lives and understanding of anyone who has an interest. We do not provide study abroad programs; we just leverage the college and university programs across the country, but there are some specific resources on our website, other websites, study abroad offices, the State Department website, and travel bureaus. I think a very good first step is to immerse yourself in the experiences of other people, and that is something we do that I don't believe anyone else does.

Our primary purpose is to serve by connecting with more students. They allow us to increase that body of knowledge through content, and they represent a primary demographic to be served.

Gen Y Project:

Online communities are an integral part of the Gen Y culture. You have essentially created a social network that links people with the common thread of studying or working abroad.

Nick:

We're about to launch a new service called Glimpse Groups. It's similar to groups that you'll find on any social networking Website, but these are specifically related to study abroad. This service enables study abroad companies to create online communities and serve them with content and other services, and to consolidate their work.

Gen Y Project:

Because of the political climate of the United States, Americans are not winning popularity contests in other countries. Do you have advice for helping Americans living abroad navigate these negative sentiments?

Nick:

It's important to understand that this is the reality, but also there is a fairly easy way of navigating it. While there is a considerable amount of anti-American sentiment abroad, that doesn't mean everybody hates Americans. There is a lot of pro-American sentiment to counterbalance it. Most people you'll meet abroad do differentiate between the United States and Americans. They may even hate the things that the United

States is doing or has done, but that doesn't mean they'll hate you as an American. People are generally pretty good about separating the two.

As an American, you will be seen as the expert, the person who's supposed to explain why the United States is doing these things. One way to respond is to say that you simply don't know why things are being done a certain way in the U.S. and that you don't completely agree with what's going on. You can take their side as well. It's also fine to disagree with them and say, "No, I think that what's being done is largely right and here's why." People are generally good about respecting those differences — at least in the experiences we've heard through our surveys and the people who communicate with us. To a large degree, those situations provide a good opportunity to educate people even if the opinions differ.

Some of the correspondents we've worked with have steered away from such discussions or said things they don't entirely believe just to avoid conflict, but that's something you have to figure out on your own.

Gen Y Project:

Some of the older generations have a tendency to hold more rigid beliefs about other countries, while Gen Y seems to be more open to connecting with people of other races and cultures. Is this trend echoed in your experience?

Nick:

Gen Yers are much more likely to be open to different beliefs, traditions, and lifestyles than older generations. We have an article on our site where one of our writers who was studying abroad was discussing politics with an older person, and they had very different opinions. However, when that discussion ended, they left it at the door and went back to being friends. I think the takeaway for the student was one of respect more than fear, regret, or anything like that.

Gen Y Project:

How are the Glimpse articles being generated? How much writing does your staff contribute to the site?

Nick:

We really only write one section called "Worldview" where we report on recent findings on a particular topic. That happens in some other sections, but all the feature content and most other sections are contributed by young people — some are Peace Corps volunteers and some are abroad for some other reason. We edit their content to make it as good as it can be. Only a select number of people make it into the print issue. Those are our very best pieces and ones that fit into a particular regional or theme for an issue.

Gen Y Project:

For students considering studying abroad, how can they best utilize Glimpse?

Nick:

I would certainly review articles from the areas and countries that interest you. Then, step beyond Glimpse and take advantage of the resources that the program providers themselves can offer. Interacting with people is an important component after you've explored the information that's out there. You can also talk to people through our Website.

The next step is reviewing programs and making a decision on a particular program. Another really great step — which you can do through www.glimpseabroad.org *— is to involve yourself in a very active community by registering on the site, by submitting your own content, whether it's by blogging, by submitting feature articles, or by participating in surveys or answering questions people have about studying, working, or living abroad.*

287 «

Gen Y Project:

These steps are also great for building career and life skills: do your homework, reach out to people, go live in the community, be an observer, and be respectful. Then, give back by sharing your stories. I think a lot of the experience you're helping create is a wonderful laboratory for young people because they get an idea of how the business world works.

Nick:

That's true, and also how the world works in general. You can't simply consume information. There are no set-in-stone answers to everything; that's something you can only answer through interaction. And, of course, your experience will be different and unique from someone else's. It's important to remember to give back to the community that helped equip you with that knowledge, so you can help someone else increase their own knowledge and understanding.

Gen Y Project:

How many people belong to the Glimpse community now?

Nick:

We have about 15,000 people who are, in some way, part of our community — whether they're donors, subscribers, or students. There are 6,000 people who are actual student contributors, and that number is always growing.

Gen Y Project:

What message can you leave with people that would convey your mission?

Nick:

I would encourage everybody to think about what we encapsulate with the tagline for the Glimpse Foundation, which is, "It's your world. Get acquainted." It's the recognition that you, as an individual, have a stake in this world because it is, in part, yours and because of this, you should know it and know it well.

POINTS FOR REFLECTION

 In order to begin learning about another country or culture, start by immersing yourself in studies about that culture. A journal such as *Glimpse Quarterly* can provide you with a starting point for your education. For more information on how to subscribe, visit http://store.glimpsefoundation.org/subscriptions.php

 Today's employers are looking closely at candidates who have studied or worked abroad. If you are a college student, contact your career office or study abroad office to learn more about internships and work study programs offered through your college or university.

 Before committing yourself to a study abroad or work study program, do your homework. Many of the private companies that offer such programs charge hefty fees. Before making a decision, contact the U.S. State Department at http://travel.state.gov/travel/living/studying/studying_1238.html

 One of the best ways to learn about a culture or a country is to live there, carefully observing and respecting the people and laws of that country. Once you have lived there, write or speak to others about your experiences.

 As Nick Fitzhugh and the team of The Glimpse Foundation say, "It's your world. Get acquainted." By traveling and studying abroad, you can open yourself up to some amazing opportunities and a wealth of information.

ABOUT NICK FITZHUGH

Nick Fitzhugh began The Glimpse Foundation as a student at Brown University, where he earned a BA in comparative literature. His prior experience spans a broad range of work: as Associate Director of Research for Building2 Partners, LLC; Vice President of Business Development for MDigital Systems; reporter for the *Cape Cod Chronicle*; Director of Public Relations and Associate Captain of the FSAE Race Car Design team; and Vice President of Capital Sap, a maple syrup company. Nick has lived in France, Italy, and Switzerland and has traveled extensively throughout Europe. He is fluent in French and Italian and served as a contributing editor to *National Geographic Traveler on Campus*. For more information on the Glimpse Foundation, visit www.glimpsefoundation.org.

» CHAPTER 24 «

PEACE TV: Mari Moss

*"I realized that if we were going to impact this
generation in any kind of positive way, we'd have
to do it through the media."*

At the age of 23, Mari Moss was earning a huge salary in New York City, working as the talent coordinator for a television show. She had gone there to escape the violence she had seen in her hometown of Canton, Ohio, where young people were dying in tragic circumstances.

Mari returned to Canton to help her mother and ended up discovering that she couldn't escape her past but could prevent a similarly violent future for other youths. Mari used her experience in entertainment to establish Present your Talents for Peace, an organization established in 2002. It provides a more healthful, positive alternative to violence, drugs, teen pregnancy, and other negative choices that teens face. Present Your Talents for Peace encourages vulnerable, at-risk youth to lead positive lives through expression in art, culture, education and the media.

She also founded PEACE TV (Positive Events in Arts Culture and Education Television), a bi-weekly television show that presents a peaceful alternative to the negative messages she was seeing broadcast on networks that were feeding the mindsets of the country's youth. She also recognizes the vital role of the music industry in shaping positive mindsets among the young followers of the hip-hop music genre.

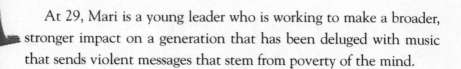

At 29, Mari is a young leader who is working to make a broader, stronger impact on a generation that has been deluged with music that sends violent messages that stem from poverty of the mind.

Gen Y Project:

What led you to establish Present Your Talents for Peace and PEACE TV?

Mari:

When I was 14, I lost my first friend to violence. It was a shock because when you're young, you think you have your whole life ahead of you. You don't expect tragedy to happen out of the clear blue sky but that's what happened to me.

We thought that was just one instance, but a year later, another young person died, and another one the year after that. It started happening more frequently, and we were just beside ourselves.

My number one goal was to get out of my community, go away to college, get a degree, and maybe one day be a savior of young people. I saw what was happening to my friends who were having kids at 14 and 16, dying, involved in drugs, and making all kinds of negative choices.

So I went off to college, got my degree in sociology, and ended up being approached by a singing group — because I also sang. We were offered a record deal and, at the same time, I was hired by a national television show working out of New York. Either way, my life was directing me into the entertainment industry. I ended up working as the talent coordinator for this popular show. My job was to call the celebrities that were coming on the show and get their contracts together. I got to meet all these celebrity producers and performers like P. Diddy, Russell Simmons, and Lil Bow Wow. I was 21, living in the big city, and just enjoying life.

I was making so much money and meeting celebrities; it was a dream job. Then my mother called and said she needed me to come home for a little while. I thought I wouldn't go back to this small town, but duty called, and I went home for a short time. I was sad to see that the situation I'd left had grown worse and another friend of mine had lost his life.

No one was doing anything about it, however. I said, "We can't just pretend that young people aren't losing their lives," and I was inspired to hold a peace rally. I'd never put on an event before. Over 1,000 people came, which showed me the community was concerned about this situation. We held a candlelight vigil in memory of those who'd lost their lives under the age of 26 — and there were hundreds.

In my little community of less than 80,000 these young people were losing their lives just left and right. That struck a chord with me.

Gen Y Project:

How did you channel this inspiration?

Mari:

We encouraged the young people there to use their talents and abilities for positive things and sponsored a talent show. We said, "There's a talent within you that you can use to do something positive instead of negative, destructive things." It was standing room only; we filled this entire gymnasium. After that event, my friend said, "Did you see what you did for this community? You've got to continue this." I said I would think about it.

I was sitting at home watching MTV and BET and I saw it with new eyes. I went outside after that and noticed kids walking and driving by, and I saw a mirror reflection of what was on the TV. I realized that if we were going to impact this generation in any kind of positive way, we'd have to do it through the media.

Gen Y Project:

What was your vision for PEACE TV?

293 «

Mari:

Our vision is to make going to school cool, making good grades cool, and making positive decisions in your life cool, just like hip-hop has made bling-bling cool. We have events that draw thousands of young people at a time. We use the media, the Internet, and music to reach young people in positive ways. Right now, we're partnering with radio stations to do a radio broadcast in convergence with television to take our show to a whole other level.

Gen Y Project:

You have a powerful message. You start locally and work your way towards solving a national concern.

Mari:

Our young people are really hurting and they're looking for answers. We're competing with choices that are coming at them every day in school and on the street. We're competing with girls' boyfriends, where they have to make a choice about sex to keep this guy.

That's why you see the influx of teen pregnancies in choices like that. We're also seeing it in the streets. Why get a job at Burger King or wherever when you can make twice that amount in a couple hours working on the streets. We're saying "Look at the big picture; see where you can be in 5 or 10 years. It's a better decision to get good grades so you can get a good job with benefits."

Gen Y Project:

You're really trying to change a cultural mindset. What influences Gen Y to shift their thinking?

Mari:

We have a lot of opportunities through our organization to help develop young people's potential in marketing, public relations, and just 21st century jobs they can put on a college resume. When you tap into young people's potential — and they realize there are opportunities for jobs other than picking up trash — they shift their thinking to using their skills in a way they can put on a college resume.

Then, we have kids who will call, email, or even post on MySpace that they feel like they just can't go on. Immediately, I take action to connect them with counselors, but if we were not there for them, I shudder to think what they would do.

Gen Y Project:

How many of these young people, once they get to you, are surprised to find they have options?

Mari:

Every one of them. We work with hundreds of young people every year. We've seen a lot of people going to college and doing bigger, better things with their lives. They're taking experiences with them that they would not have otherwise. They get a whole new sense of reality. They put their creativity and their own knowledge to work in a way that's going to empower them. It's just an amazing thing to see.

Gen Y Project:

Understanding that there is a choice to go down either path seems like the first level of awareness. What can people do at any level that would help support your efforts?

Mari:

Our goal is to go national but we need the funds to have the impact we want. This just started out in a 22 year-old's mind five years ago and it's been growing ever since. We've done a lot with less than $10,000 a year. Kids are signing up hundreds at a time, so it's the sign that people are getting this. If we had the funding, imagine what we could do.

Gen Y Project:

How can you use the media and Internet to help with your objective?

Mari:

Hip-hop is so influential and this music includes a lot of negative messages. We need to get more positive words and images in this music because this music is destroying the generation. It's like a giant monster, but there are people with a lot of power and influence who are partnering to stop that. One thing we're doing is joining with the local hip-hop radio station and converging our message through television and radio. When we do events, the only talent that can come on our stage is positive talent. That's starting from a smaller scale.

Gen Y Project:

We've also got to shift the desire in the people who are producing this music to understand that they can still win and be successful by doing it in a positive light.

Mari:

That's what I saw so clearly at 23 when I realized that if we can flip this whole genre into being something positive, then we can impact this generation in a great way.

Gen Y Project:

Who are some of the people you respect in the hip-hop industry? We want to know who is help making hip-hop positive and cool?

Mari:

There are a lot of rappers out there that could have a positive message. For example, Kanye West has had some positive songs come out, but we really have to get back to the days of Queen Latifah. Every one of her songs was positive, never negative. It was about women respecting themselves. Then we have a big group of rappers who are giving contradictory messages. For example, Ludacris right now has a very positive song out called "Runaway" with Mary J. Blige, but if you look into some of his early music, it wasn't so positive.

Gen Y Project:

As long as those records and videos are selling, it's going to be hard for the industry to say, "We're not going to go along with this." How can we influence them to reconsider?

Mari:

The music industry is all about sales. My feeling is you have to get to the root of a problem in order to solve it. The whole root of this situation is poverty — and not just that you can't pay bills or put food on the table; it's poverty of the mind. We've got to get young people, especially in the inner cities, involved with positive activities where they can put food on the table. We've got to change the language in the record industry; we've got to empower the young people and get their minds on more positive messages, period.

Gen Y Project:

Do you have plans for reaching your goals?

Mari:

One of the ideas that I had for a major fundraiser is a peace tour with performers who want to spread this positive message — who want to stand up against horrible things that are happening to our young people, like the Virginia Tech tragedy. Having these artists go from city to city on this tour would raise the money to really catapult this effort.

Gen Y Project:

What's the biggest project you're working on right now?

Mari:

We're working on developing opportunities to give young people summer jobs. We want to be able to get them ready to do internships, summer jobs, and so on. We're giving them incentives to be off the streets.

The other current project is finalizing deals with regional hip-hop radio to do a convergent piece and get young people signed up for the summer opportunities program.

Gen Y Project:

The whole Gen Y mindset holds the belief that a great vision brings about collaboration. You're bringing more consciousness and choice to the younger generation, a group that will be taking care of the older generations.

Mari:

You've got to think of the big picture, 25 years ahead of the game. We have to start developing our youth right now and we can't make excuses for why we can't be involved. I want everyone to think about the future generation. We need to get them ready to carry on the legacy. I want to look at how we can impact this generation through the media, music, and the Internet and impact them in a positive way.

POINTS FOR REFLECTION

 Everyone has a specific purpose and reason for being on this earth. It is up to you as a unique individual to discover your talents and tap into your potential to live your dreams and make positive change. As you do, you will create a ripple effect that will reach other people and help change the world for the better.

 Generation Y is the future and your future is now. There is no need to wait to make a positive change or to make a difference in the world. All it takes is passion, commitment, persistence, and dedication. Start now.

 As a Generation Y leader, you can affect the change and respect you want to see in the world by taking part in the political process.

 You have an amazing amount of knowledge, creativity, and skill. Use them to reach others and teach others, and to make positive things happen in the world.

 Generation Y will set the tone for generations to come. If you take a passive approach, the next generation will follow your lead. If you take an active approach, the following generation will be active and involved. You have a golden opportunity to design the environment for future generations. Embrace that power so you can set the proper stage for the generations to come.

ABOUT MARI MOSS

Mari Moss abandoned a promising entertainment career following the shooting death of a friend and moved back to her hometown of Canton, Ohio, to combat violence. She is the founder and executive director of Present Your Talents for Peace, a non-profit organization showcasing the talents of Stark County youth. Mari is also a volunteer producer and director of PEACE TV (Positive Events in Arts Culture and Education Television), a youth oriented broadcast program. Her efforts provide young people with positive alternatives to gang violence, drug abuse and other risky behaviors. Mari's vision is to be a positive inspiration to young people and encourage them to make positive changes in their lives. To learn more about Mari Moss or to make a donation to her causes, visit www.youtube.com/PEACETV or contact Mari at 330-412-1644.

» CHAPTER 25 «

Digital Gangster: Eric Green

"A lot of people think we're in the information age, but we're really not. We're in the communication age."

Technology is one of the greatest gifts bestowed on Gen Y. With the Internet and all the tools that have accessorized it, young people have seized myriad online communication tools and zoomed past the older generations, leaving all others in a dense cloud of dust.

While Gen Yers readily grasp the latest, greatest, and coolest sites, software, and gadgets, this world can be intimidating to those outside of Gen Y. Throughout this book, we have tried to close up the communication gap between generations. The ability to use these Web tools presents a gaping hole, so we thought we'd wrap up our discussions with a gift of knowledge for those who aren't totally clued in to digital technology.

We asked Eric Green for clarity. Also known as the "Digital Gangster," Eric is a Gen Xer who focuses on unraveling the mystery of Web technology, one site and one network at a time. He is tuned into video, the next wave of social networking technology, and provided us with a primer.

Technology doesn't have to be complex to be useful. The simpler it is, the bigger the community. Like so many other discussions before this, you just have to understand the rules if you want to play the game.

Gen Y Project:

Eric, video has exploded as the hottest digital technology. What new dimension has the visual impact brought to the Generation Y network?

Eric:

The power of video is amazing. People typically retain about 10 percent of what they read, 20 percent of what they hear, but 50 percent of what they see and hear. Together, the information and the message in video are so much more powerful than other mediums out there, so the learning that Generation Y is achieving using this medium is most definitely deepening their learning.

Gen Y Project:

You can use this for social networking, but isn't it also a valuable business marketing tool?

Eric:

Yes. This medium is my favorite marketing tool because it gives me a chance to use video not only to promote myself, but to set me up as more of an authority. Between YouTube and about 30 to 40 other networking sites out there, video sites get about a billion views a week — it's just astonishing.

Gen Y Project:

I've seen a wide range of videos online, some are very basic and others appear professionally produced. How can a newcomer to this technology create something that will be noticed?

Eric:

The viewing audience is going to want to know that you're being yourself. They don't need you to have a super professional video, but they need to feel that you created this yourself. If it's this very high level, professional video, the public will not connect with you like they will on a pretty basic level.

Gen Y Project:

Interesting. We've heard that creating video is not complicated, but I'm sure a lot of people are skeptical. To begin with, can you give us a little bit of the down and dirty nuts and bolts of the equipment you're going to need?

Eric:

To do a screen capture, all you would need is a simple microphone. There's free software out there to handle the rest. I would suggest you go to www.camstudio.org. That's a simple download and will allow you to capture whatever is happening on the screen.

Full motion video is something I encourage and all you need to do that is a simple webcam. A lot of computers come with the microphone built in, but, if not, there are webcams as low as $50 that have the built in mic, and, just like a printer, you download your drivers and then plug in your device.

To edit the video — if you're using a PC, you could use something as simple as Windows Movie Maker, which is free. If you don't already have it on your computer, you can simply download it. Really, that's it in the way of hardware that you would need.

Gen Y Project:

What about tutorials? Are there online resources for more information on using the software and various platforms, like MySpace?

Eric:

There are some video tutorials online which will show you how to set up a MySpace account, how to use Windows Movie Maker, and give you a

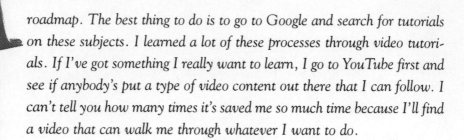

roadmap. The best thing to do is to go to Google and search for tutorials on these subjects. I learned a lot of these processes through video tutorials. If I've got something I really want to learn, I go to YouTube first and see if anybody's put a type of video content out there that I can follow. I can't tell you how many times it's saved me so much time because I'll find a video that can walk me through whatever I want to do.

Gen Y Project:

I'm also really big on learning by doing. With all of these tools available, is it true that if you can type, you can use these platforms?

Eric:

Yes, and there are even websites out there with MySpace templates so you can spruce up your page if you want. Just don't get caught up into thinking that every word has to be perfect. You've just got to get it out there. You can't stop with one video either. It's just like blogging…if you are going to start using video, I recommend that you create a short two-minute video every other day and post it so that you build a viewing audience.

Gen Y Project:

How about the content of the videos: are there some basic rules for how much information you want to convey in a video?

Eric:

If you've got something you want to get across, be concise and give them a call to action. You also want to break information down into parts. Say you break something into four parts, and someone sees part three; if they like it, they'll go seek out the other parts, believe me.

Gen Y Project:

Once you've created your video, how do you get it onto the Web?

Eric:

*Let's start with MySpace. You simply create a YouTube account —
which is free — create your video, and then upload your video to it.
You can then use the link from YouTube on your MySpace account,
on your blog and on a variety of video listing sites on the Internet.
You can set your video up under a specific topic or title, and then use
specific tag words or key words. I would encourage you to take a look
at YouTube, and really find out what key words are going to attract
your target market*

Gen Y Project:

*You often hear teens talking about MySpace. Is it really the best choice
for others to build an online social network?*

Eric:

*For many years, I thought MySpace was just a social networking site for
teenagers or college students to connect with one another. I was wrong.
MySpace has over 250,000 new members joining every single day and I
think numbers are now over 200 million that are part of that online social
network. These are people from around the world that are connecting
with one another.*

Gen Y Project:

*With so many people there, where do you begin to break into this huge
community?*

Eric:

People treat the Internet as a big billboard and they need to throw their name up with the other millions of names. One of the strategies we teach is something called "My Story Marketing" and it's very effective. A lot of the online communities have not gotten this.

Gen Y Project:

Can you explain how "My Story Marketing" works?

Eric:

Let's say you're at a networking event and you're a real estate agent. You walk in, jump on a table and say, "Hey everybody, I'm Eric Green. I'm a real estate agent with Farnsville Morrisey and we have the best rates in town. You should do business with me." People would look at you like a guy who's off his rocker and you wouldn't last too long. They'd probably escort you out the door.

What you should do is walk in, connect with somebody: "Hi, I'm Eric. I'm originally from Florida..." And you're building rapport before you get into business. That's how MySpace needs to be treated as well. It's a huge opportunity to connect with people and promote your products, services, and business, but when you tell your life story, you have a way to connect to people.

So when they go to your page and you've got four different sites you're try-ing to promote — or just really slapping them in the face, so to speak — with your business, products, and services, that's going to turn them off.

Gen Y Project:

So you suggest a more subtle approach to using MySpace to build your social network?

Eric:

Implementing My Story Marketing and using MySpace can really start building a huge network to promote whatever you want. The software that we use is called <u>www.addnewfriends.com</u>. It's an automated system where you can send what they call "friend requests" to people on MySpace who you want to join your group. It would literally take forever if you were just searching one at a time, so what you do is categorize the groups you really want to target and invite that group to join your MySpace group.

As people are starting to come into your network, they're looking at your page, and if it's set up correctly, people are going to connect with your story and that might drive them to an additional page where you have additional information about your product or service.

Gen Y Project:

I followed your instructions, and I actually hand-selected some groups based on my profession. I've had close to 50 people in two days sending me emails saying "It's so nice to meet you. It sounds like we have a lot in common…" It's really easy and effective.

Eric:

Yes…it is easy. If the site were difficult to go in and set up, there wouldn't be this many people joining. You just need to decide you want to do this, get out there, put that up, and start building that network.

Gen Y Project:

Let's move on to another site that has been a huge factor in the viral video phenomenon: YouTube. This platform has raised the bar significantly for communication. How has YouTube altered the way we use the Internet?

Eric:

A lot of people think we're still in the information age, but we're really not. We're in the communication age. People will be contacting you, not the other way around, and I'm reaching out to people to try to tell my story and get them to buy into me.

Gen Y Project:

The whole goal is to develop relationships with people, get them to know you, and do it consistently. The next thing you know, the phone rings and someone wants to talk to you about your services.

Eric:

I can't tell you how powerful that is. By implementing this system, these videos are working for me 24 hours a day, seven days a week. I'm giving a call to action, and if they like what they've heard and they connect with me, then they want to contact me and make sure that I'm real. When you begin to experience that, it's very empowering.

Let me give you an example. My partner out in Australia, John Gregory, put a very simple video together with just some music, motivational quotes, and pictures. He wasn't promoting anything. Today, that video has about 100,0000 views. The power in that video is that tacked on to that is information about John Gregory and what he's promoting — his online business, or whatever he's passionate about.

That cost him not one cent to upload that video to YouTube and then transfer that to the other social networking sites as well.

Gen Y Project:

That's inspiring! The ability to use this tool is definitely within our reach. Can you talk about another platform, Hello World?

Eric:

Hello World is a video enabled, social networking platform, with only about 35,000 members at the moment. However, they do offer a number of different things — one is video email. It's a web-based email platform and it's the only one where you can send both video and text emails.

You can also brand the email and put in specific banners that link to websites — very powerful when you're connecting to people. If somebody sends me an email, then I'll reply to that individual with a short video email. It's amazing the kind of reaction I get from that, like "Wow, that was cool!" Again, you're allowing video to build rapport.

Gen Y Project:

Are there other aspects of Hello World that are valuable?

Eric:

A couple others are videoconferencing; you can connect with up to four people live, right over the PC. It's like IM'ing — and I use it to have live video chats with people that I'm partnered up with.

The other part of this platform that's extremely powerful is the live video webcasting. Through this, you have the ability to launch your own live, video webcast and anybody who can access Hello World, can see your webcast listed on Hello World TV, and click onto it. Those broadcasts can also be archived, so people can go back and re-watch that information.

It's an extremely powerful tool that can be used in all sorts of ways once you open your mind to whatever you do, whatever you're passionate about, or whatever you promote.

Gen Y Project:

Are these tools geared primarily toward business use?

Eric:

They're designed for the masses. It's very user friendly. It could be a business user, or it could be a grandmother who wants to connect with friends and family across the world. When you go to <u>www.helloworld.com</u>, they'll also help you generate code so you can put videos right on your website. Then you can take that link from your website and put it all over the Internet.

Gen Y Project:

Gen Y is using this process and these platforms like nobody's business. If you're trying to connect with a younger audience, this is the way to go. Eric, you're very passionate about this subject. Has it changed the way you approach communication?

Eric:

My mindset has changed completely. Now I'm thinking of ways I can give people content that will help somebody, or help promote what I'm talking about. I'm not thinking about who I'm going to call or who I'm going to go see. I'm just a guy in Apex, North Carolina. I'm telling my story, and people will connect with that and some people won't.

POINTS FOR REFLECTION

 Educate yourself on the power of video — such as video email, live web casting, video blogging — as a communication tool. This will allow your audience to connect with you through the personal touch that video delivers and they will retain more of your message.

 Set up your own video channel with one of the most powerful video social networking sites on the planet today, YouTube. This video site garners right now over a billion video views a week.

Set up a MySpace page that brands yourself and join over 200 million other people around the globe in one big networking party.

 Learn the power of My Story Marketing and how to apply this approach both online and in face to face interactions. This method will absolutely explode your network because people do business with people they know, like, and trust. People will do business with you first if they know they are buying "you" as a part of the package.

 Don't wait for your competition and the world to realize the power of video as a communication and marketing tool. Take action now to distinguish yourself in the marketplace before everyone climbs on board with online video.

ABOUT ERIC GREEN

Web 2.0 Specialist **Eric Green** — a.k.a. "The Digital Gangster" — has been in the world of corporate sales for over 12 years. After struggling for over five years to figure out a way to leave Corporate America and pursue his dream of becoming an online entrepreneur he's finally cracked the code. Today Eric consults with entrepreneurs around the globe and teaches them the latest in web 2.0 strategies to brand themselves and build wide-spread networks. To learn more about Eric Green, visit www.myspace.com/thedigitalgangster.

Y

» ADDITIONAL RESOURCES «

Far additional free resources, including links, articles and references on

⭐ Choosing the college of your choice

⭐ Applying for college scholarships and financial support

⭐ The top blogging, video and social networking sites

⭐ Finding the internship and/or career of your dreams

⭐ Marketing to Generation Y

⭐ And much much more!

Visit: **http://millennialleaders.com/resources**

Check out what books your authors and Coaches recommend and continue learning more about Millennial Leaders.

And **REMEMBER — tell a friend about this book!** People will always remember the first person that turned them on to a cool tool or new trend in the marketplace.

Be that person.

Printed in the United States
95324LV00007BB/1-6/A